The Gourmet's Guide to Quick Cuisine

Unconventional Culinary Creations

By

Lisa R. Fraser

GAME.

Game must not be soaked in water and it should be washed only when necessary and then quickly dried. The flavor of game depends greatly on its preparation, the latter makes it one of the finest dishes. Game ought to be fried and roasted; boiled game is never as savory.

Butter, bacon and cream are the best fats in which to fry game. Sweet-sour victuals are best to serve with game as: Red cabbage, apple sauce, currant jelly and Cumberland sauce.

No. 1—ROAST SADDLE OF VENISON.

Quantity for 6–10 Persons.

1 saddle of venison
Salt
1 pinch of pepper
Bacon for larding
1 pt of sour cream, good measure
1 tsp. of lemon juice
1½ tbsps. of flour
½ cupful water
½ lb. of butter

Preparation: The deer, fawn or doe must hang in its skin a few days before it is cooked. The neck is cut off. The ribs are chopped off if they are too long. The skin is taken off, the meat pounded and larded closely with bacon strips; place a thin slice of bacon under the fillets. Fry the venison on both sides with part of the ½ lb. of butter, put the rest of the butter into the pot or pan and roast the meat 45 minutes, basting frequently with the sour cream. The roast should be pink inside and very juicy. Put it on a hot platter and prepare the gravy.

Stir the flour into the frying butter, brown it a few minutes, add the water, cook 5 minutes and add the lemon juice, then strain.

Remarks: The remnants of this venison may be utilized in a soup. Fry them with some butter or lard and soup greens and a tablespoonful of flour, add water and cook slowly for two hours. For directions refer to No. 63 and 64 under Soups, Chapter 1.

No.2—LEGOFVENISON.

Quantity for 6 Persons.

1 leg of venison, 3½ to 4 lbs.
Salt
¼ lb. of butter
½ qt. sour cream
⅛ lb. of bacon cut in wide, thin slices, for lining the pan
1 tbsp. of flour
½ cup of water
⅛ lb. bacon strips

Preparation: The meat is pounded on both sides, washed, dried, skinned and larded with bacon. The joint of the leg is chopped. Scald the leg with a pint of boiling water and place it into the hot butter in the roasting pan, brown it on both sides, then place the bacon slices on the bottom of the pan and the leg of venison on top of them, roast in the oven for one hour, basting it often with spoonfuls of cream.

The Gravy: After the leg of venison is done, stir the flour into the drippings, brown it for 2 minutes, then add the water, cook for 5 minutes and strain.

Remarks: With a tablespoonful of red wine you can improve the gravy. If you wish to have the meat rare, allow ¾ hour for roasting. Add or subtract some of the time for frying according to the size of the piece of venison.

No.3—VENISONCUTLETS.

2½ lbs. of venison from back or loin
Salt
Scant ⅛ lb. of butter

FortheGravy .

⅛ lb. of butter
3 tbsps. of flour
1 qt. of water
¼ pt. of Madeira
Some soup greens
1 pinch of sugar
Salt
1 clove
1 tsp. of meat extract
½ tsp. of lemon juice
1 pinch of pepper

Preparation: The meat is skinned, cut into ½ inch slices, each having a rib bone, then they are pounded on both sides and salted. Chop the scraps and fry them with the soup greens, light brown in hot butter, stir in the flour and brown it, add the water and season with salt, pepper, sugar, lemon juice, Madeira and clove and cook slowly for 1½ hours. Strain the gravy and put into it the meat extract and truffle slices and stew a little while. The cutlets are fried 4 minutes in the ⅛ lb. of butter; serve on a hot platter and pour the gravy, which should be smooth, over it.

Remarks: You may also pour tomato or champignon gravy over the meat. The platter with the cutlets would look well garnished with puff paste scallops.

No.4—DEERORDOELIVER.

Quantity for 2 Persons.

1 deer or doe liver
Salt
1 pinch of pepper
⅛ lb. of butter
1 tbsp. of chopped onion
2 tbsps. of vinegar
2 tbsps. of water
½ tsp. of meat extract
½ tbsp. of flour

Preparation: The liver is washed and dried. Trim off the membrane, cut into even thin slices, salt and pepper and fry quickly in the hot butter. Onion and flour are stirred in and stewed with the liver. Then the water, vinegar and meat extract are added and cooked well; when done, serve at once because the liver will get hard and tough when standing.

No.5—VENISONRAGOUT .

Quantity for 6 Persons.

3–4 lbs. of venison
¼ lb. of butter
4 tbsps. of flour
1½ qts. of water
½ onion, sliced
6 pepper-corns
2 cloves
1 bay-leaf
Juice of ½ lemon
1 tumblerful of red wine
Salt

Preparation: The meat is cut into 3 inch squares. The ¼ lb. of butter is browned with the flour, then water is added and all the spices and cooked 5 minutes. The meat is put into this gravy, the pot well covered and ¼ hour before done, the red wine is added. If the gravy has boiled down too far, add some more water. When the ragout is done, take out the meat, strain the gravy and pour it over the meat, serve on a hot platter. The gravy should be smooth. This meat should be cooked in an iron pot.

Remarks: Potato dumplings are nice with venison ragout.

No.6—T OCAR VEALEGOFVENISON.

Leg of deer, doe or reindeer may be carved like a leg of veal. From the leg, remove first the skin and membrane and you will recognize the parts called the fricandeaux. On top of the leg lies a flat piece, on the side of it a piece that has the shape of a small fillet. These pieces may be used for fricassee or they may be filled and roasted. You may leave these pieces on the leg and lard and roast it with them. The tail end is chopped off, chopped in small pieces, and with the last ribs which are attached to it, a soup is cooked.

Remarks: All uncooked game keeps in vinegar or milk.

No.7—SADDLEOFVENISON.

Quantity for 14–16 Persons.

1 saddle of venison, 8 to 10 lbs.
Salt
¾ lb. of butter
¼ lb. of bacon for larding
1 pt. sour cream
1 tsp. of lemon juice
2 tbsps. of white wine
6 pepper-corns
2 cloves
2 tbsps. of flour
1 cup of water
1 tsp. of meat extract, if necessary

Preparation: The joints are chopped in several places so the meat lies flat in the pan, then it is skinned, washed, larded well, salted and fried on both sides in the hot butter; then put into the oven with all the spices and left to roast for 2 to 3 hours, basting frequently with the sour cream.

For the gravy, stir in the flour, brown it a little, then add the water and cook with the roast for 15 minutes. Strain the gravy and if the color is too light, add the meat extract.

No.8—LEGOFVENISON.

Quantity for 14–18 Persons.

1 leg of venison, 10 lbs.
Salt
6 pepper-corns
2 cloves
¾ lb. of butter
1 pt. of sour cream
2 tbsps. of flour
1 cup of water
1 tsp. of lemon juice
2 tbsps. of white wine
¼ lb. of bacon for larding

Preparation: The preparation is the same as described in No. 7, only the time for frying is longer, from 3 to 3½ hours.

Remarks: If the meat is from an old animal, it is best to keep it in milk, wine or vinegar for 2 to 3 days.

No.9—ANOTHERFORMOFLEGOFVENISON.

Quantity for 14–18 Persons.

1 leg of venison, 10 lbs.

Salt
Some melted butter
Rolled out bread dough
1 sheet of paper

For the Gravy.

¼ lb. of butter and ¼ lb. of drippings
Salt
1 clove
3 pepper-corns
2 tbsps. of flour
Bouillon cooked from remnants
1 tumblerful of port wine

Preparation: The meat is skinned, the bone trimmed out, washed and salted. A sheet of paper buttered or brushed with fine salad oil, is wrapped around the meat, then it is enveloped in a layer of white bread dough. Heat ¼ lb. of drippings and ¼ lb. of butter, place the leg of venison into it and roast for 5 to 5½ hours, basting it often. Remove paper and crust, when done, and brush the meat with gravy.

The gravy is prepared by browning the flour in the drippings, adding all the spices, the port wine, and the bouillon, then cooking it well. If the gravy is too greasy, skim it off and strain before serving.

Currant jelly or apple sauce is served with this meat.

No. 10—CHOPPED STEAK OF GAME.

Deer, Doe, Boar or Wild Rabbit Meat is Used.

Quantity for 6 Persons.

3 lbs. of meat
¼ lb. of bacon
⅛ lb. butter
Salt

1 pinch of pepper
Scant ½ lb. of butter for frying

FortheGravy .

1 tbsp. of flour
3 tbsps. of cream
1 tsp. of lemon juice
½ cup of water
1 tbsp. of capers

Preparation: The membrane and tendons are removed from the meat, then it is chopped or ground fine together with the bacon and mixed well with ⅛ lb. of butter, salt, pepper and shaped into steaks.

The other portion of butter is heated and in this the steak is fried 10 minutes on the stove, basting and turning often. Put it on a hot platter and prepare the gravy.

If there is too much drippings left, take some out, stir in the flour, brown a few minutes, then add all the ingredients and cook well, pour it over the steak, serve immediately.

No.1 1—COLDGAMEPIE.

MadeFr omDeer ,Doe,BoarorRabbitMeat.

A good way to utilize the remnants of game roasts.

Quantity for 6 Persons.

2 lbs. fried or roasted game
¼ lb. of butter
Salt
1 pinch of pepper
2 soaked rolls
1 tsp. of grated onion
¼ lb. of truffles, sliced
4 eggs

¼ lb. finely chopped sardines
2 soaked rolls
Some butter for the dish
¼ lb. finely grated Parmesan cheese

Preparation: The meat is chopped or ground very fine. The butter is melted—add to it the rolls, chopped sardines (from which the bones have been removed) and onions, one whole egg and 3 yolks of eggs. This mixture is stirred on the stove and left to stew until dry.

After cooling it off, add the chopped meat, salt and pepper. Press the whole through a sieve so there will be no chunks or pieces. Into this mass stir the truffle slices, the beaten whites of eggs, and the Parmesan cheese.

Fill a buttered dish or casserole with this mixture, cover it, set it in a steamer over a kettle of boiling water and boil 1½ hours. After cooling, turn it out on a platter, garnish the platter with prepared lettuce. This makes a fine dish for an evening dinner.

Remarks: This pie may also be served hot; then serve a game gravy or herb gravy with it.

No.12—GAMERAGOUTMADEFROMREMNANTS.

Quantity for 6 Persons.

1½ lbs. cold game remnants, either deer, doe, rabbit or wild boar meat
⅛ lb. of bacon
1 tbsp. of butter
2½ tbsps. of flour
1½ tbsps. of lemon juice
1 small onion
Salt
1 pinch of pepper
1 pt. bouillon, boiled from the bones
½ cup sour or sweet cream
2 vinegar or dill pickles, sliced

Preparation: The meat is cut from the bones in nice, equal pieces. The bones are brought to boil in 2 qts. of cold water and boiled down to 1 pt. of broth or bouillon.

Cut the bacon into cubes and brown it in the butter, onion slices and flour and add the bouillon. If you have left over game gravy, add that too, season with salt, pepper, lemon juice and cream and cook slowly for 20 minutes, then strain and cut the pickles into it. Put the meat pieces into this gravy and let it get hot, but do not cook or the meat will get tough. The gravy must be smooth. After heating, serve at once.

Remarks: If you wish to have the ragout very fine, omit the pickles and take truffles or champignons instead.

No.13—LEGORSADDLEOFWILDBOAR.

Quantity for 14–18 Persons.

10–14 lbs. of wild boar meat

ForPickling.

5 qts. of vinegar
10 pepper-corns
1 doz. juniper berries
1 large onion, sliced
3 cloves

ForFrying.

1 bottle of red wine
Salt
1 qt. of bouillon

ToCovertheRoast.

1 lb. grated rye bread
½ lb. of butter

3 tbsps. of sugar
4 pulverized cloves

FortheGravy .

3 tbsps. of flour mixed with some water
1 tsp. of meat extract

Preparation: The roast is pounded, the surface scored or cut in squares and the meat placed into a deep pot or jar. Vinegar, pepper, juniper berries, cloves and onion slices are put in and left with the meat for 3 days. After this time take the roast out and roast it in a deep roaster with all that was on it in the jar, except the vinegar. Instead of that, pour on the red wine and bouillon, season with salt and roast in the oven for 3½ hours. Then strew the roast with rye bread crumbs which have been mixed with ½ lb. of butter, pulverized cloves and 3 tablespoonfuls of sugar. Roast it 30 minutes longer so the crust will get hard and brown. In the meantime add the flour mixed with water to the gravy and cook it a while, then strain, add the meat extract, cook again, taste for salt and spices and skim off the fat.

Remarks: The remnants of roast are utilized in the same way as those of pork roast.

No.14—HOWT OSKINARABBIT .

Hang the animal up by its hind legs on two nails, rip the rabbit from tail to throat, lengthwise. Take out the insides, cut the bile carefully from the liver, retain the latter and the heart and lungs, and throw away the rest of the intestines. Now separate the fur skin from the inner skin, make a cut through the fur around each ankle, pull the legs through, cut off the ears and pull the whole fur skin down from the hind legs over the head.

No.15—RABBITROAST .

Quantity for 4 Persons.

1 rabbit
⅛ lb. bacon for larding
Salt
1 pinch of pepper
½ pt. sour or sweet cream
1 tsp. of lemon juice
1½ tbsps. of flour
1 cup of water
Scant ½ lb. of butter

Preparation: The dressed rabbit is washed and dried, head, throat and the skin from the belly and its fore paws are cut off and the joints of its hind paws are chopped. The back and legs are larded with thin slices of bacon. The butter is heated and the larded hare is placed into it to roast for 45 minutes. Season with salt and pepper and baste frequently with cream. If it is an old hare, it will require 1¼ hours for roasting. Ten minutes before the hare is done, add the lemon juice and the flour and stew 5 minutes, then pour in the water, leave the hare in this gravy 5 minutes longer, then serve it with the strained gravy.

No.16—STEWEDRABBIT .

Quantity for 4 Persons.

1 rabbit
¼ lb. of butter
⅛ lb. of bacon
2 cloves
2 cups of rye bread crumbs
½ bottle of red wine
Salt, pepper

Preparation: The rabbit is prepared as described in No. 15, well larded, cut into pieces large enough for each person. The forelegs may be larded too. These pieces are fried in ¼ lb. of butter until they are light brown. Now pour the drippings into a deep roasting pot, add the bacon slices and make a layer of hare meat, season with salt, pepper, cloves and put on 1 cup of rye bread crumbs. Over this pour the red wine. After making another layer of meat and bread crumbs, cover the pot well and stew slowly 2 to 2½ hours. Serve the meat on a hot platter, strain the gravy, flavor and pour it over the meat. If the pot cannot be closed tightly, paste a strip of paper or cloth around the rim and cover.

Remarks: Potato dumplings are good with this meat.

No.17—ANOTHERFORMOFSTEWEDRABBIT .

Quantity for 4 Persons.

The preparation is the same as given under No. 16 with the exception of taking ½ pt. of sour cream instead of wine and 2 tablespoonfuls of flour instead of rye bread crumbs.

The hare is prepared and cooked the same as given under No. 16. If the gravy is too thick, add more water.

No.18—RABBITCUTLETS.

Quantity for 4 Persons.

1 rabbit
Salt
1 pinch of pepper
2 eggs
1 small piece of bacon
Grated wheat bread for breading
1 egg
Some melted butter

FortheGravy .

½ pt. broth
1½ tbsps. of flour

⅛ lb. of butter
Juice of one lemon
½ tsp. of sugar
Salt
1 wineglassful of red wine

Preparation: All meat is cut from a well dressed rabbit, skin and membrane removed; the bacon and meat are chopped or ground fine, seasoned with salt and pepper and mixed well with 2 eggs and small cutlets formed. The butter is heated, the cutlets brushed with it, then dipped into the bread crumbs and finally into the beaten egg. Some ribs are cut off the skeleton and stuck into each cutlet. The butter for frying is put into a pan, heated and the cutlets fried to a nice brown color. The gravy has been prepared by browning the heart, liver and lungs in 1½ tablespoonfuls of flour, then adding 1 pt. of broth or water, putting into this all the bones and seasoning with salt, cloves, and 4 pepper-corns. Cook the gravy for ½ hour and add the red wine or port wine, lemon juice and sugar. Strain and serve with the cutlets. Garnish the platter with currant jelly.

No.19—HASENPFEFFER(RABBITPEPPER).

Quantity for 2–4 Persons.

The head, neck, breast, lungs, forelegs, heart, liver, 1 lb. of rabbit meat or lean pork
Some vinegar
1 small onion
⅛ lb. of bacon or butter
3 tbsps. of flour
Salt
4 pepper-corns
2 cloves
1 bay-leaf
2 pts. of water
1 tbsp. of sugar
½ cup of red wine (or not)

Preparation: The head, neck, breast, lungs, heart, liver and forelegs are cleaned well, cut in medium large pieces and left in vinegar for 1 day.

After the rabbit has been fried, cut 1 lb. of pork into medium large pieces. Cut the bacon into small cubes and fry it, or if you use butter, heat this and fry the finely sliced onion and pork in it and the rabbit meat which has been soaked in vinegar.

For the gravy, stir the flour into the drippings, stew a few minutes, then add water and all the spices and other ingredients. Then slowly cook the meat until tender in the gravy. When it is done, take the meat out and serve on a hot platter, strain the gravy and pour over the meat.

Remarks: You may omit the rabbit meat and pork and use only the heart, lungs, liver, head, neck, breast and forelegs if these are sufficient. You may also stir a little vinegar into some rabbit blood and add to the gravy. The liver may be omitted and fried separately.

No.20—RABBITLIVER.

Quantity for 1 Person.

1 rabbit liver
1 pinch of salt and pepper
1 well-beaten egg
Some flour
1 piece of butter for frying
1 slice of lemon

Preparation: The liver must be very fresh. As soon as the rabbit is shot, dress it, take the liver out and prepare it the same day. If you cannot do this the same day, it is better to leave the liver and prepare it with the rabbit.

The fresh liver is washed, sliced, seasoned with salt and pepper, dipped into egg and flour, then fried quickly in some hot butter and served at once on a hot platter. Place a lemon slice on it.

No.21—RABBITROASTSALAD.

Quantity for 6 Persons.

¾ lb. of bare roast
3 medium-sized, boiled potatoes
2 hard-boiled yolks of eggs
2 raw yolks of eggs
¼ pt. fine salad oil
Wine vinegar according to taste
1 tsp. of mustard
Salt
1 pinch of pepper
1 tsp. of capers
1 tsp. of sugar
¼ cupful of cream

Preparation: The meat and potatoes are cut into small pieces. The 2 hard-boiled yolks of eggs are mixed well and stirred with the 2 raw yolks, the oil dripped in, cream, vinegar and the other ingredients mixed in. Taste the gravy and stir lightly into it the meat and potatoes, then heap it in a glass dish, chop the 2 whites of eggs and strew over the salad.

No.22—RABBITPIE.

2 young rabbits
1 piece of bacon for larding
½ lb. chopped pork
1½ rolls
2 eggs
Salt
1 pinch of pepper
1 tbsp. of butter for the filling.

ForFrying.

¼ lb. of butter
3 tbsps. of flour
1½ qts. of water or bouillon
1 small onion
¼ bottle of white wine
1 bay-leaf
6 pepper-corns
1 clove
Lemon peel
1 small can of truffles, sliced

Preparation: Shoulders and legs are cut off and the rest of the meat removed from the bones and chopped very fine, also the pork. Mix this well with the soaked rolls, eggs, butter, salt and pepper.

Line the bottom and sides of the dish with this mixture. The meat from the loins of the rabbits is cut into nice pieces, fried brown in ¼ lb. of butter and put into the pie with the sliced truffles.

Now prepare the gravy. Into the butter in which the pieces of meat have been fried, stir 3 tablespoonfuls of flour, brown and add 1½ qts. of water or bouillon. Season it with all the spices, onion, salt, bay-leaf, pepper, clove, lemon juice, white wine and the truffle peelings and cook slowly for 1 hour. Strain the gravy and pour ¾ of it into the pie, put on another layer of the filling, bake in medium hot oven for 1½ hours or cover the dish well and set it in a steamer over a kettle of boiling water and boil 1½ hours. The remainder of the gravy should be served hot with the pie.

Remarks: The bones are chopped up and broth cooked from them which is used for the gravy to make this rich and palatable.

Remarks: This, pie may be served cold.

No.23—DOMESTICRABBITROAST .

Quantity for 4 Persons.

1 domestic rabbit

⅛ lb. of bacon
⅛ lb. of butter
½ cup of sour or sweet cream
1½ tbsps. of flour
½ cup of water
Salt

Preparation: The domestic rabbit is prepared and cooked the same as described under No. 15, Rabbit Roast.

No.24—STUFFEDDOMESTICRABBITROAST .

Quantity for 4–6 Persons.

1 domestic rabbit
⅛ lb. of bacon
⅛ lb. of butter
½ cup of sour or sweet cream
1½ tbsps. of flour
½ cup of water
Salt

ForStuffing.

Heart, liver, kidneys of the rabbit
2 soaked rolls
2 eggs
1 tbsp; of butter
1 tbsp. of lemon juice
Salt, pepper, nutmeg

Preparation: The domestic rabbit is prepared like the rabbit under No. 14, but the legs, neck and breast are left on, because it is going to be stuffed. It is washed well inside and outside and salted. Heart, liver and kidneys are chopped fine and mixed well with the soaked rolls and the other ingredients. The rabbit is filled with this stuffing and sewed up, the back well larded and fried on all sides light brown in hot butter. Then it is roasted in the oven for 1½ hours, basting frequently with the cream and lemon juice.

Remarks: The domestic rabbit may be made into ragout. See No. 5, Doe or Deer Ragout.

Remarks: The stuffing may be improved by adding champignons or truffles or ¼ lb. of chopped pork.

No.25—LAPINS.

Lapins, the European hare, are prepared like rabbit. See No. 23 and No. 24.

FISH.

THE VARIOUS PREPARATIONS OF FISH AND THE UTILIZING OF REMNANTS.

Every fish has a season when it is most savory. During the breeding or spawning season, no fish is good. When you buy a dead fish, observe carefully the following:

1. The meat of the fish must be firm and must not show any form of decay, neither in smell nor taste.
2. The skin must be tight on the fish.
3. Both eyes must be clear, not milky or sunken.
4. The gills must be red and slimy. Fish frozen very hard are not especially good.

The meat of middle sized fish is more savory than that of large ones.

When you buy live fish, take the lively ones, not those that swim on their side or back. The bought fish are best killed in the market. The quickest way of killing a fish is to stun it with a blow on the head or neck, then cutting its throat and its tail.

You scale the fish by taking hold of its tail and with a sharp knife or fish scaler scraping off the scales from there towards the head.

To retain the nourishing qualities of the fish, it is not soaked in water, only washed and boiled immediately. Whole fish are put on the fire with cold or hot water. Pieces of fish are put on with boiling water or prepared in hot butter or lard to retain the nutriment in the fish, since the hot water or fat contracts the cells at the cuts. The skin of a whole fish retains the nutriment, therefore it may be put on the fire in cold water.

Fish must not be covered up while cooking or frying so that the temperature will not get too high. Frozen fish must be thawed completely before using; if this is not done, the inside of the fish is mostly rare when serving it. No dish will be good when the fish or meat used is prepared in a frozen state.

Fish are dressed by making a slight cut along the whole under side and taking out all intestines. The inner darker membrane must be entirely removed and the fish washed well.

No. 1—TO BOIL.

Whitefish, shellfish, pike, codfish, pickerel, bass, black bass, white bass, flounders, plaice or sole, carp, salmon, trout, brook trout, cabeljou, river trout.

Quantity for 6 Persons.

3½–4 lbs. of fish
4 qts. of water
Salt
10 pepper-corns
4 cloves
1 large onion
2 bay-leaves
½ lemon, sliced

Preparation: The fish is dressed and washed. Into a fish kettle pour 4 qts. of water, all the spices and enough salt to make it quite salty. Place the fish on the tray of the kettle in a swimming position and bring slowly to boil 5 minutes in cold or hot water, then set back to draw ½ hour. When the meat near the gills is not bloody any more, the fish is done. Before serving, rinse it with hot water to remove the scum and place on the platter in a swimming position. It is then garnished with lemon slices, parsley, lettuce and potatoes.

With the fish is served a fish gravy, mustard gravy, Bearnaise gravy or fresh creamed butter, browned butter, mustard butter, parsley butter, etc.

No. 2—BAKED FISH.

Any of the varieties named in No. 1.

Quantity for 6 Persons.

3½—4 lbs. of fish
¼ lb. of fresh butter
Salt
3 pepper-corns
Some flour
1½ cups of sour or sweet cream
¼ tsp. of meat extract
Juice of ½ lemon
1 tbsp. of capers
1 tbsp. of Parmesan cheese

Preparation: The fish is dressed, washed and dried, salted inside and outside and rolled in flour. It is placed into a pan or if possible an earthen or porcelain dish in which the butter has been heated; then put into the oven and baked for 10 minutes to a light yellow color. Baste with the cream and lemon juice, sprinkle with the Parmesan cheese, and add the capers and pepper-corns. In this gravy stew it ½ hour, then prepare carefully on a hot platter and serve. Strain the gravy through a sieve to remove all lumps, i.e., make it smooth. If it is too thick, add some cream or milk and pour it on the fish or serve it extra.

Remarks: This preparation is very fine. A little meat extract makes the sauce look more delicate.

No. 3—FISH STEAMED OR STEWED IN RED WINE GRAVY.

Any one of the varieties named in No. 1.

Quantity for 6 Persons.

3½–4 lbs. of fish

Salt
⅛ lb. of butter
3 tbsps. of flour
1 pt. of water or bouillon
1 pt. of red wine
1 tsp. of meat extract
½ onion, sliced
3 slices of lemon
½ carrot, sliced
Small piece of celery root
1 small piece of parsley root
6 pepper-corns
2 cloves
2 bay-leaves
1 tbsp. of sugar

Preparation: The fish is dressed, washed, dried, salted inside and outside and left in a cold place for 1½ hours. The gravy is then prepared. Brown the butter and flour and mix in all the ingredients, also red wine; add water or bouillon and cook slowly 1½ hours and strain. It must be smooth and palatable.

Rub the salt off, put the fish into a porcelain or earthen dish in which the ounce of butter has been melted and roast in the oven for 10 minutes, basting frequently with the butter. After this, pour the gravy over it and stew the fish uncovered in the oven for ½ hour.

Remarks: The pan or dish should not be much larger than the fish, so that this is well covered with the gravy. Both fish and gravy are served on the same hot platter.

No. 4—BROILED OR ROASTED FISH.

Any one kind named in No. 1.

Quantity for 6 Persons.

3½–4 lbs. of fish

Salt, flour
½ cup of roll crumbs
¼ lb. of butter
1 beaten egg

Preparation: The fish is dressed, washed and dried, then ripped lengthwise into two halves and the bones removed. Then salt, dredge with flour, dip into beaten egg and roll in bread crumbs. Drip melted butter on the fish, place into a flat pan and roast or bake in the oven, basting with melted butter. Serve with brown butter gravy and garnish with lemon slices.

No. 5—BOILED SALMON.

Quantity for 6 Persons.

3 lbs. of salmon
3 qts. of water
½ cup of vinegar
1 cup of white wine
1 large onion, sliced
2 tbsps. of salt
1 tbsps. of pepper-corns
10 whole cloves
3 bay-leaves
½ lemon, sliced

Preparation: All ingredients are put into the water and then boiled. The fish is not scaled, but the insides taken out and washed. When the water boils, set it aside, put the fish in and let it draw ½–¾ hours. Cooking would make it tough. Serve a butter or madeira gravy with the fish.

Remarks: If the fish is a salmon, it requires 20 minutes to cook it.

No. 6—SALMON, BLUE.

Quantity for 15 Persons.

7 lbs. of salmon
7 qts. of water
¾ bottle of white wine
1 cup of wine vinegar
1 tbsp. of pepper-corns
6 cloves
3 bay-leaves
1 onion, sliced
1 lemon, sliced
1 piece of carrot
1 piece of celery root
1 piece of parsley root
⅛ lb. of butter
¼ cup of salt

Preparation: The is dressed, washed and dried. The vinegar is heated and poured on the fish, then it is placed into a fish kettle in a swimming position and the water is poured on cold, so that it almost covers the fish. All the ingredients are added; bring it to boil and set aside to simmer 1 hour. The fish must be served carefully and garnished with parsley and lemon slices; potato balls are good with it. For gravy, serve creamed butter, drawn butter, egg gravy, remoulade gravy or mayonnaise dressing.

Remarks: Salmon is good served cold with a mayonnaise dressing.

No. 7—SALMON SALAD.

Quantity for 6 Persons.

2 lbs. of salmon
2 hard-boiled eggs
1 raw yolk of egg
Fine salad oil
1 tsp. of mustard
Juice of 1 lemon
1 tbsp. of vinegar
1 tsp. of sugar

Salt
1 pinch of pepper

Preparation: The boiled fish is arranged on a glass dish in a mound after being cut into nice pieces and the bones removed. The gravy or dressing is made by stirring the raw yolk of egg into the boiled yolks, adding the oil a few drops at a time, also the lemon juice, vinegar and the other ingredients. It must be thick. The dressing is poured over the salad and slightly mixed with a wooden spoon. Garnish the salad with hard-boiled eggs and green lettuce leaves.

No. 8—SLICED SALMON BROILED.

Quantity for 6 Persons.

2½ lbs. of salmon
Salt
¼ cup melted butter
1 tbsp. of finely sliced onion
1 bunch of parsley
⅛ lb. of butter for frying
2 tbsps. of lemon juice

Preparation: The salmon is cut into 2 to 3 slices, cleaned, washed and dried well. Brush the slices with the ¼ cup of melted butter, salt and put on the lemon juice, onion slices and parsley. Cover the dish and put on the stove for one hour but do not fry. After one hour, put into a broiler, broil for 10 to 15 minutes, basting with butter and turning frequently. You can also fry them in a buttered pan. Serve in a hot dish, garnish with lemon slices and parsley and serve with a tomato or olive gravy, or a cold, sour gravy.

No. 9—BOILED SALMON TROUT.

Quantity for 6 Persons.

3½ lbs. of salmon trout
Water enough to cover the fish
Salt
¾ pt. of vinegar
10 pepper-corns
2 cloves
1 bay-leaf
½ onion, sliced

Preparation: The fish is cleaned and washed. The water with all ingredients in it is brought to boil, the fish placed into it in a swimming position, cooked 10 minutes and served on a hot platter. A fish or egg gravy may be served with it.

No. 10—FRIED TROUT.

Quantity for 6 Persons.

3½ lbs. of trout
Salt, flour
1 beaten egg
¼ lb. of butter

Preparation: The fish is dressed, washed, dried, salted inside and outside, dipped into the beaten egg and then into flour. The butter is heated in a pan, the fish fried in it to a light brown color and a butter gravy served with it.

No. 11—EEL, BLUE.

Quantity for 6 Persons.

3½ lbs. of eel
1½ qts. of water
6 tbsps. of vinegar

10 pepper-corns
2 bay-leaves
4 cloves
½ sliced onion
½ sliced lemon
Salt
Water for cooking

Preparation: The eel is killed by wrapping the head into a cloth and giving it a few blows with a hatchet; then rub it with salt from head to tail until it looks blue. Skin the eel by making a cut in the skin around the head and pulling this down over the tail; if it does not strip off easily, cut it loose with a sharp knife. Cut the fish into equal pieces and clean each piece separately, pushing out the intestines and inner membrane and rubbing it with salt.

1½ qts. of water is brought to boil with 4 tablespoonfuls of vinegar and the eel scalded with it. Heat fresh water, 2 tablespoonfuls of vinegar, pepper-corns, bay-leaves, cloves, 1 onion, lemon slices and salt; in this water the eel is cooked slowly 15 minutes. The fish is then served on lettuce leaves and garnished with lemon slices. Caper, mustard or remoulade dressing is served with it. This fish is good eaten cold.

Remarks: The remnants of eel may be used to make aspic or head cheese. The eel broth and skin are utilized for it. See Head Cheese and Gelatines, No. 9 Eel in Jelly.

No. 12—BAKED EEL.

Quantity for 6 Persons.

3½ lbs. of eel
Salt
1 pinch of pepper
1 beaten egg
Flour for dredging
¼ lb. of butter or lard for frying

Preparation: The eel is prepared as described in No. 11. The bones are taken out of the pieces, (these may be 3 to 4 inches long) salt and pepper, roll in beaten egg and flour and bake in hot butter to a nice brown color.

A Dutch dressing may be served with it.

No. 13—EEL IN BEER.

Quantity for 6 Persons.

3½ lbs. of eel
3 tbsps. of butter
2 tbsps. of flour
1 qt. of white beer
½ onion, sliced
¼ lemon, sliced
Salt
1 pinch of pepper
1 clove
½ bay-leaf

Preparation: The eel is prepared as in No. 11, the bones being removed from the pieces. The 3 tablespoonfuls of butter are stirred into the flour, the beer added and also all the spices and lemon and onion slices. Cook this gravy and put in the pieces of eel to boil 20 minutes. Serve the eel on a hot platter, strain the gravy and pour it over the eel. The gravy must be thick and very palatable.

Remarks: If the gravy is not thick enough, mix some more flour with water, stir it in and let it boil.

No. 14—EEL WITH RICE. (FRICASSEE).

Quantity for 6 Persons.

3½ lbs. of eel

⅛ lb. of butter
2½ tbsps. of flour
1 pt. of cream
Salt
Juice of 1 lemon

Preparation: The eel is prepared according to No. 11, cut into 4 inch pieces and cooked almost done in boiling water, salt, 2 tablespoonfuls of vinegar, ½ sliced onion, 8 pepper-corns, 2 cloves, 1 bay-leaf. When almost done, take out the pieces and put them into the gravy, which is prepared in the following way: Heat the butter, stir in the flour, add the cream and stir well until smooth, add salt and lemon juice and let it simmer 10 minutes. Serve eel and dressing on a hot platter and place a rim of cooked rice around it. Then strew over the whole some fine minced parsley. If you wish you may sprinkle chopped parsley over the eel before serving, or you may cook the parsley in the dressing.

Remarks: The gravy must be smooth and savory.

No. 15—COLD EEL ROULADE.

Quantity for 6 Persons.

3 lbs. of eel
4 hard-boiled, chopped eggs
1 tbsp. of chopped parsley
1 tbsp. of chopped capers
Juice of one lemon
Salt, pepper
½ tbsp. of chopped onion

For Cooking.

2 qts. of water
10 pepper-corns
3 cloves
1 bay-leaf

1 small piece of carrot
1 small piece of parsley root
1 small piece of celery root
Salt
½ onion

Preparation: The eel is prepared as described in No. 11, its head and tail cut off and ripped open lengthwise; intestines and bones carefully taken out; then cut it in two crosswise, to make 4 pieces. These pieces are washed, dried and rubbed with salt. The four hard boiled eggs are chopped and mixed well with the chopped parsley, onion, capers, lemon juice, salt and pepper. This stuffing is put inside of the four pieces of eel and these rolled up tightly and tied with string, then each tied up in a piece of white cloth. Into the 2 qts. of water put all the ingredients for cooking, and the head, tail and skin chopped up into small pieces and cook 15 minutes. This eel stock must be tasted as to seasoning, vinegar added and the prepared pieces of eel cooked in it slowly for 45 minutes. Leave them in the stock until pretty well cooled off, then take them out and place them between two platters. After a few hours, take off the strings and cloth and cut them into thin slices which are served on green lettuce leaves and garnished with hard-boiled eggs. You may serve them also with pickles and mayonnaise or mustard dressing.

Remarks: These eel roulades may be made into eel jelly. See Chapter Nine, No. 9.

No. 16—LARDED PICKEREL.

Quantity for 6 Persons.

3½ lbs. of fish
⅛ lb. of bacon
Salt
1 pinch of pepper
¼ lb. of butter
1 tbsp. of flour
¾ pt. sweet or sour cream
½ tsp. of meat extract

1 tbsp. of Parmesan cheese
Juice of ½ lemon
1 tsp. of capers

Preparation: The fish is dressed, washed, dried and rubbed with salt inside and outside. The back is skinned by slitting the sides and pulling the skin off. The back is then larded with bacon strips. The butter is heated in a pan and the fish placed into it in a swimming position after dredging with flour and grated Parmesan cheese. The hot butter is dripped on, also the lemon juice, and the fish put into the oven to bake 15 minutes. During this time baste with the butter carefully so the flour and cheese make a crust on the fish. Gradually add the cream and capers, and bake the fish in this dressing for ½ hour, basting frequently. Serve on a hot platter. Color the gravy with the meat extract and if it is too thin, add 1 teaspoonful of flour, mixed with cream or milk, cook and strain. The gravy is served with the fish; garnish with potatoes and macaroni and serve with sauerkraut.

No. 17—LARDED AND STUFFED PICKEREL.

Quantity for 6 Persons.

3½ lbs. of fish
⅛ lb. of bacon
Salt, pepper
¼ lb. of butter
tbsp. of flour
1 pt. sour or sweet cream
½ tsp. of meat extract
1 tbsp. of Parmesan cheese
Juice of ½ lemon
1 tsp. of capers.

The Stuffing.

1 pt. can of champignons
2 tbsps. of butter

½ cup of sweet cream
Salt, pepper
1 tbsp. of flour

Preparation: The preparation is the same as given in No. 16. The filling or stuffing is made from chopped champignons stewed in the butter, flour, salt, pepper and cream. This is stuffed into the fish which is then sewed up. The fish is larded and cooked according to directions in No. 16. The gravy is also prepared as in No. 16.

No. 18—STUFFED AND LARDED PIKE.

Quantity for 6 Persons.

The preparation and ingredients are the same as given under No. 16 and No. 17.

No. 19—FISH FRICASSEE FROM PICKEREL OR WHITEFISH.

Quantity for 6 Persons.

1 pickerel or whitefish, 3½ lbs.
⅛ lb. of bacon for larding
¼ lb. of butter
1 cup of cream

For the Fricassee.

18 crabs
2½ qts. of salt water
1½ lbs. veal sweetbreads
Juice of ½ lemon
Salt, pepper
⅛ lb. of butter
20 champignons

10 peeled truffles
2 tbsps. of butter
1 tbsp. of lemon juice

Preparation: The fish is dressed, washed, dried, the skin taken off the back and this larded with bacon. Then it is sprinkled with salt and put into a pan in a swimming position with ¼ lb. of butter and 1 cup of cream and fried slowly for 1 hour to a golden yellow color. During this time simmer the 18 crawfish or crabs in salt water for 45 minutes. They should not boil, but simmer. From eight crabs take out the meat and leave the other ten whole.

The veal sweetbreads are scalded, the membrane removed, salted and peppered, the lemon juice dripped on, then dredged with flour and fried in ⅛ lb. of butter to a nice brown color. The sweetbreads are cut into nice pieces. The champignons are heated in 1 tablespoonful of butter; lemon juice, salt, pepper, 2 tablespoonfuls of cream are added. The truffles are peeled and sliced and stewed with ½ tablespoonful of butter, 3 tablespoonfuls of bouillon, 1 pinch of salt. The crab meat from the 8 crabs is chopped fine and stirred with 1 tablespoonful of butter and 1½ tablespoonfuls of flour; add a little cream and boil. The lemon juice, salt, pepper and 1 yolk of egg are stirred in and set to cool. Small dumplings are formed from this mixture and fried in hot lard. The batter for the dumplings must be thick; try one first and if it does not hold together, add more flour. These small dishes must be prepared while the fish is cooking. That which is done must be kept hot in hot water. The fish, when done, is served on a hot platter in a swimming position, three crabs are placed on the fish's back, the other seven along its sides. The pieces of sweetbread are also arranged neatly around the fish and the champignons and truffles, as well as the fish dumplings. All must be very hot and kept so until the gravy is done.

The Gravy: Into the butter in which the sweetbreads were fried stir some flour and add bouillon or water, pour it into the pan in which the fish was fried and cook for 2 minutes, taste and strain. It must be smooth and be served with the fish.

Remarks: This is a fine dish for parties. Potato balls and green lettuce are served with it.

No. 20—PICKEREL WITH TOMATO SAUCE.

Quantity for 6 Persons.

3½ lbs. of pickerel, white fish or cod fish
Salt
1 sheet of paper
⅛ lb. of butter, good measure

Gravy.

⅛ lb. of butter
⅛ lb. of ham
6 tomatoes
3 tbsps. of flour
2 tbsps. of Parmesan cheese
Salt
Pinch of pepper
½ pt. bouillon
½ pt. of cream

Preparation: The fish is dressed, washed, dried, salted, placed into a pan and lightly covered with a buttered paper. Then the hot butter is poured over it and it is cooked in the oven until well done, basting frequently for about one hour. In the meantime the gravy is prepared thus: The ham is cut into small pieces and fried light yellow in the butter, with onion slices and flour, then add bouillon and cream, season with salt, pepper and add Parmesan cheese; also put in the sliced or chopped tomatoes and cook until pretty thick. Strain the gravy, taste it and heat it again. The fish, which must be a nice pink color, is brushed with the thick gravy and served in a swimming position. The rest of the gravy may be served separately.

No. 21—PICKEREL OR CODFISH SALAD.

Quantity for 6 Persons.

1¾ lbs. of pickerel or codfish

2 tbsps. of butter
1 scant tbsp. of flour
1 small onion
1 pt. thick cream
2 yolks of eggs
1 tsp. of mustard
2 tbsps. of vinegar
1 tbsp. of salad oil
Salt
1 pinch of white pepper
1 tbsp. of capers

Preparation: The boiled fish is cut up into nice pieces. The butter is melted, the peeled whole onion fried light yellow in it, then taken out. Stir in the flour, add the cream and cook 5 minutes. The 2 yolks are stirred in, but the gravy must not cook any more, cool it and season with salt, mustard, pepper, capers, vinegar and salad oil. Pour the gravy over the fish.

No. 22—BAKED RED SNAPPER.

Quantity for 6 Persons.

3½ lbs. of red snapper
Salt
1 beaten egg
Some flour
1 cup of rolled crackers
¼ lb. of butter

Preparation: The fish is dressed, washed, dried and rubbed with a little salt. It is then dredged with flour, dipped into the beaten egg and cracker crumbs. The butter is heated and put on the fish, then baked in the oven for ½ hour until a nice brown. Serve a parsley gravy with it.

No. 23—PICKEREL OR WHITEFISH WITH SAUERKRAUT.

Quantity for 6 Persons.

1 lb. boiled pickerel or whitefish
1 lb. boiled sauerkraut
1 egg
1 large piece of butter
¾ pt. of cream
Some salt

Preparation: A baking dish or casserole is buttered and filled with layers of sauerkraut and fish alternating. The bones must have been removed and the fish cut into nice pieces. There should be 3 layers of sauerkraut and 2 layers of fish. After the dish is filled, stir the cream with some salt and pour over the whole. Put a little butter on top and bake in oven for 45 minutes.

No. 24—BOILED TURBOT.

Quantity for 6 Persons.

3½ lbs. of fish
Salt
½ qt. of wine vinegar

Preparation: The turbot is drawn by making a cut across the dark side below the gills, then rub it with salt until all slime is gone. After washing it, pour ½ qt. of vinegar on and let it stand for ½ hour. Run the knife along the spine on the black side and slit the white side in several places to prevent the skin from bursting while cooking. Fins and tail are shortened. Put plenty of salt water into the fish kettle, put the fish in, white side up, and cook slowly for 5 minutes, then set aside to simmer for ½ hour. Do not cover up the kettle. When serving, the white side should be up and garnish the platter with any kind of lettuce or salad i.e., cucumber salad, head lettuce or endive. Place lemon slices on the fish or small boiled crabs. Serve with a butter gravy or creamed butter and potato balls.

No. 25—TURBOT FRICASSEE.

Quantity for 6 Persons.

1 lb. of fish remnants
A small calf's tongue
½ pt. of champignons
1 tbsp. of capers
3 tbsps. of butter
½ pt. of cream or milk
Juice of ½ lemon
Salt, pepper
½ pt. of bouillon
2 tbsps. of Parmesan cheese
2 tbsps. of flour

Preparation: The fish is cut into large pieces. A baking dish is buttered and the pieces of fish placed in. Add 3 tablespoonfuls of heated butter, stirred with 2 tablespoonfuls of flour, the cream, champignon juice and bouillon. The latter may be omitted. Cook the gravy until it is smooth and add the lemon juice, salt, pepper, chopped champignons and capers.

The tongue which has been boiled is skinned and sliced and put into the gravy, then boiled a few minutes and tasted as to seasoning. Pour this gravy over the fish, strew with Parmesan cheese and drip on some butter. Place the baking dish into a dish with water and bake in the oven to a nice color.

No. 26—BOILED RED SNAPPER.

Quantity for 6 Persons.

3½ lbs. of fish
Salt

10 pepper-corns
4 cloves
2 bay-leaves
½ onion, sliced
½ lemon, sliced
Water

Preparation: The fish is dressed, washed and put in a swimming position, into water enough to cover it and brought to boil. All the ingredients are added and after boiling up once, set aside to simmer ½ hour. Garnish with lemon slices and parsley. Serve the fish with a butter gravy mixed with fine chopped parsley or with an egg dressing.

No. 27—RED SNAPPER WITH RED WINE DRESSING.

Quantity for 6 Persons.

The preparation and ingredients are the same as given under No. 3.

No. 28—FRIED SMELT OR SPARLING.

Quantity for 6 Persons.

3½ lbs. of sparling
Salt
1 egg
2 tbsps. of milk
Flour
½ lb. of butter for frying

Preparation: The fish is dressed, washed, rubbed with salt and left standing for 1½ hours. Then the salt is washed off a little. Beat the egg with the milk, brush the fish with it and dip it into the flour. Heat the butter and bake the fish in it in the oven to a nice brown color.

When served, pour the drippings over.

No. 29—FILLET OF SHELLFISH, WHITEFISH, CABELJOU, SOLE, WITH DRESSING.

Quantity for 6 Persons.

3½ lbs. of fish
¼ lb. of butter
Salt, pepper
Juice of 1 lemon

Fish Bouillon.

Bones, skin
4 pepper-corns
2 cloves
1 bay-leaf
2 slices of lemon
½ onion
1½ qts. water
Salt

Preparation: The fish is dressed, washed, the bones all removed and cut into equal fillets. These are salted a little and left with the salt ½ hour.

During this time prepare the fish bouillon. The bones and skin are brought to boil in 1½ qts. of water to which the pepper-corns, cloves, lemon and onion slices and salt have been added and then cooked until the water has boiled down to ¾ qt. Then put the fish fillets into a buttered pan, season with 1 pinch of pepper, lemon juice, the ¼ lb. of butter placed on in pieces and ½ cupful of the fish bouillon poured over them.

The pan must be covered and the fish stewed in the oven for 25 minutes, then served on a hot platter, the drippings poured over. A Dutch gravy is served with it and the bouillon used for that. See gravies or dressings, Dutch Dressing.

No. 30—FRIED MACKEREL.

Quantity for 6 Persons.

3½ lbs. of mackerel
Salt
1 egg
2 tbsps. of milk
Flour
½ lb. of butter for frying

Preparation: The mackerel is cleaned well, the head chopped off and the fish split open lengthwise. The bones are all taken out, the fillets rubbed with salt and let stand for 1 hour. Then it is washed a little, dried, dipped into the egg beaten with milk and into flour. The butter is heated and the fillets are fried in it to a nice color for about 10 to 15 minutes. Serve on a hot platter, pour the drippings over and garnish with lemon slices and parsley. If the drippings are not sufficient, make an extra gravy of drawn butter mixed with chopped parsley.

No. 31—ROLLED, STUFFED FISH FILLETS.

Made from whitefish, pickerel, cabeljou, shellfish, halibut.

Quantity for 6 Persons.

3 lbs. of fish
1½ rolls, soaked in milk
1 tbsp. of chopped parsley
½ tbsp. of chopped onion
1 pinch of salt
1 pinch of pepper
3 eggs
⅛ lb. of butter

For Stew.

½ pt. of white wine
1 oz. of butter

6 pepper-corns
¼ onion
2 lemon slices
3 tbsps. of lemon juice

The Gravy.

⅛ lb. of butter
2 tbsps. of flour
¾ pt. of fish gravy
3 yolks of eggs

Preparation: The fish is dressed, washed, skinned, split open lengthwise and the bones taken out, then it is cut into pieces 6 inches long and 3 inches wide. The trimmings which are left, must be fully ¼ lb. and are chopped fine. From 2 eggs make scrambled eggs. Cream the ⅛ lb. of butter and mix it well with the soaked roll, chopped fish trimming, 1 tablespoonful of parsley, scrambled egg, onion, salt, pepper. Press the whole mixture through a sieve and stir in another egg. This stuffing must taste very spicy or piquant and is spread evenly on the fish fillets. Then roll each one up and tie it with a white string, place them into a roasting pan, add ½ qt. of water, ½ pt. of white wine, 6 pepper-corns, ¼ onion, 2 slices of lemon, 3 tablespoonfuls of lemon juice and salt. The 1 ounce of butter is cut into pieces and put on the fish, then cover the pan with a buttered paper and bake in the oven ½ hour. Serve on a hot platter.

The gravy or dressing is prepared by mixing ⅛ lb. of butter with 2 tablespoonfuls of flour, add the strained broth from the fillets, cook and stir in 3 yolks of eggs, strain and serve with the fish fillets.

No. 32—BOILED CODFISH.

Quantity for 6 Persons.

3 lbs. of codfish
⅛ lb. of soda
2 onions

Salt
4 qts. of water

Preparation: The fish is pounded well, and put into water for 36 hours, changing it every 12 hours and adding a teaspoonful of soda at every change. After that, skin the fish and cut it into pieces, place it into boiling water with the salt, and 2 sliced onions, and let it simmer for 45 minutes. Serve it with drawn butter or mustard gravy.

No. 33—CODFISH RAGOUT.

Quantity for 6 Persons.

1½ lbs. of boiled codfish
⅛ lb. of butter
2 tbsps. of flour
¾ pt. of bouillon
6 pepper-corns
2 bay-leaves
Salt
A small cup of herb vinegar
½ onion

Preparation: The remnants of boiled codfish are cut in small pieces. The ⅛ lb. of butter is browned, 2 tablespoonfuls of flour stirred in, add the bouillon and season with vinegar, onion, pepper-corns and bay-leaves.

The gravy is cooked slowly ½ hour, seasoned and strained. Add the fish, reheat but do not boil and serve on a hot platter with potatoes.

No. 34—FRIED SOLE.

Quantity for 6 Persons.

3½ lbs. of fish
Salt, white pepper

1 egg
2 tbsps. of milk
1 cup grated rolls
Juice of 1 lemon
1 onion, sliced thin
¼ lb. of butter for frying
Some flour

Preparation: Skin the fish by running a sharp knife around the tail; loosen the skin from the meat and pull downward over the head. The white side is treated the same way, the tail and fins are shortened and the fish cut into convenient pieces. Every piece is cleaned well, salted and peppered, the lemon juice dripped on, the slices of onion placed on top, the pot covered up and the fish left in it to simmer 1½ to 2 hours. ½ hour before serving, each piece is dried, dredged with flour and dipped into the egg beaten with the milk and salt and then into roll crumbs.

The butter is heated and in it the pieces of fish are fried to a nice brown color. Serve it on a hot platter, garnish with lemon slices and parsley. The drippings may be used as gravy.

No. 35—BAKED SOLE.

Quantity for 6 Persons.

The ingredients and preparations are the same as in the preceding, No. 34. The pieces of fish are put into boiling hot lard deep enough so they float, and baked to a golden yellow color.

Serve with a mayonnaise or caviar gravy. See Gravies or Dressings.

Remarks: The pieces of fish may be rolled in finely chopped or ground hazel nuts instead of bread crumbs; this is very fine.

No. 36—BAKED GURNET.

Quantity for 6 Persons.

3½ lbs. of fish
Salt
1 egg
2 tbsps. of milk
Juice of 1 lemon
¼ lb. of butter

Preparation: The fish is cleaned well, dried, cut in halves, lengthwise, the bones taken out, salted, seasoned with lemon juice, dipped into egg beaten with milk and then into flour.

Heat the butter and fry the fish in the oven for ½ hour, basting frequently. Serve a butter dressing with it.

No. 37—SMALL FISH RAGOUTS IN SHELLS OR SMALL MOLDS; UTILIZING REMNANTS OF FISH.

Quantity for 6 Persons.

1 lb. of boiled fish
1 oz. of butter
2 tbsps. of flour
½ pt. of sweet or sour cream
Juice of ½ lemon
1 tbsp. of Parmesan cheese
3 tbsps. of white wine
Salt, white pepper
2 tbsps. of roll crumbs
1 small piece of butter

Preparation: The butter is heated, the flour stirred in, also the cream, wine and lemon juice and boiled. This gravy should be thick; if too thick, add more cream or milk, salt, pepper and Parmesan cheese, then boil one minute. Cut the fish into small pieces and put into the gravy. Butter the shells or molds and fill with this mixture, strew the bread crumbs on and bake in the oven about 10 minutes, to a light yellow color. Serve immediately after taking out of the oven.

Remarks: This dish may be served as a fine side dish together with head lettuce.

No. 38—FISH CROQUETTES.

Quantity for 6 Persons.

1 lb. of boiled fish
1 oz. of butter
3 tbsps. of flour
¾ pt. of cream
3 yolks of eggs
1 tbsp. of. lemon juice
Salt
1 pinch of pepper
2 whites of eggs, beaten with 1 tbsp. of milk
Flour
Lard enough for frying

Preparation: The fish is cut into small pieces. The butter is melted, the 3 tablespoonfuls of flour stirred in, then add cream and season with lemon juice, salt and pepper. This gravy is cooked a few minutes and must be thick, the 3 yolks of eggs are stirred in and the fish added. After this mixture has cooled off, small croquettes are formed which are dipped into the white of egg and flour or bread crumbs. Heat the lard to the boiling point, (it must be deep enough so the croquettes will float in it) and bake them to a golden yellow color.

Remarks: Fry one croquette first; if it should not hold together, add more flour.

No. 39—FISH CUTLETS.

Quantity for 6 Persons.

The preparation and ingredients are the same as under No. 38. Form small cutlets, bread them the same as the croquettes and fry them in butter to a nice color. You may improve them with champignons or crab tails.

No. 40—FISH AND POTATO PUDDING.

Quantity for 6 Persons.

1½ lbs. of boiled fish
3 lbs. potatoes
1 pt. of cream or milk
⅛ lb. of butter
2 tbsps. of Parmesan cheese
Salt, pepper
1 tbsp. of capers
1 tbsp. of roll crumbs
2 tbsps. of flour

Preparation: The boiled fish is cut up fine, the bones all taken out; the raw potatoes peeled and sliced fine. The baking dish or casserole is buttered and a layer of potatoes alternating with a layer of fish put in so that the last layer will be potatoes.

The gravy is made by heating the butter, stirring in the flour, adding the cream, salt, pepper, Parmesan cheese and capers. Cook one minute, then pour over the layers of fish and potatoes. Strew a few bread crumbs on top and place the pieces of butter on, then bake slowly 1½ hours. Serve in the dish with head lettuce.

No. 41—SALTED CODFISH CROQUETTES.

Quantity for 6 Persons.

The preparation and ingredients are the same as given under No. 38, Fish Croquettes. If the codfish is too salty, soak it in water a few hours or simmer in boiling water a few minutes.

No. 42—CODFISH HASH.

Quantity for 6 Persons.

1½ lbs. of codfish
1 small piece of butter
1 tbsp. of flour
½ pt. of cream

Preparation: The codfish is picked to pieces. If it is too salty, soak it a few hours. Heat the butter, stir in the flour, cream and fish and cook for 10 minutes. Toast slices of wheat bread and serve the fish hash on this.

No. 43—FRIED FRESH HERRING.

Quantity for 6 Persons.

12 fresh herring
Salt
½ lb. of butter or lard
1 cup of flour

For the Gravy.

Juice of 1 lemon
⅛ lb. butter
1 tbsp. parsley

Preparation: The head of the herring must have a yellow color, if it looks reddish, the herring is stale. The herring is dressed, washed, salted for 45 minutes, then it is dried and rolled in flour, that has been mixed with salt and pepper. Heat the butter or fat and fry the herring in it to a nice color, turning occasionally. For the gravy, brown the butter, add the juice of the lemon and finely chopped parsley.

Serve the herring on a hot platter and pour the gravy over it.

No. 44—TO MARINATE OR PICKLE FRIED HERRING.

Quantity for 6 Persons.

12 fresh herring
Salt
1 cup of flour
½ lb. of butter or lard

For Marinating.

¾ qt. vinegar
¾ qt. water
1 large onion, sliced
6 cloves
6 bay-leaves
Some Salt
20 pepper-corns

Preparation: The herring are dressed, washed, salted for 45 minutes; after that they are dried, then rolled in flour mixed with salt and pepper and fried in butter or lard to a nice color.

For marinating, boil vinegar, water, pepper, cloves, bay-leaves, sliced onion and salt and cool it. The fried herring are cooled and put into a stone jar and the fluid poured over. To be prepared one day before serving.

No. 45—MARINATED SALT HERRING.

Quantity for 6 Persons.

6 salt herring
1 pt. sour or sweet cream or milk
2 sour apples
12 pepper-corns
4 cloves
2 bay-leaves
Vinegar to taste
1 small onion

Preparation: The salt herring are soaked for one day, then dressed and skinned. If you wish, you may cut them into pieces or leave them whole and put them into a dish. The gravy is then prepared.

The milt and roe, taken out of the herring, are well cleaned, chopped and beaten with vinegar, cream, grated apples and onions, pepper, cloves and bay-leaves. Pour this dressing over the herring and let stand for ½ to 1 day. Serve the herring in the gravy and potatoes in their jackets.

Remarks: Sour cream is best to use for marinating salt herring. This preparation is very good.

No. 46—MARINATED SALT HERRING.

A Simple Way.

Quantity for 6 Persons.

6 salt herring
1 pt. wine vinegar
1 large onion, sliced
12 pepper-corns
6 cloves
2 bay-leaves

Preparation: The herring are dressed, skinned and soaked in water for ½ day, then cut into desirable pieces or left whole. Cook the vinegar with ½ pt. of water and cool. Put all the spices on the herring and pour the cold vinegar over. The milt may be put in also.

No. 47—HERRING SALAD.

Quantity for 6 Persons.

3 salt herring
15 boiled, peeled potatoes
3 apples

¼ lb. cold roast
⅛ lb. tongue sausage
¼ lb. pickled beets
2 salt pickles
2 pepper pickles
1 onion
1 tsp. mustard
4 tbsp. of oil
1 pinch of salt
Pepper
1 pinch of sugar
Vinegar to taste
½ pt. bouillon
3 hard-boiled eggs

Preparation: The herring are soaked in water for ½ day, then dressed, skinned, the bones taken out, and cut into equal parts. Potatoes, apples, roast, sausage, eggs, onion, pickles, beets are all cut up, mixed well and seasoned with oil, salt, pepper, mustard, sugar and vinegar, then bouillon added. The salad is served in a glass dish and garnished with minced white of egg, yolk of egg, pickles and beets. You may also garnish with sardines cut in halves and rolled.

No. 48—BOILED LOBSTER.

Quantity for 6 Persons.

3 lobsters, 2½ lbs.
Boiling water
Salt
12 pepper-corns

Preparation: The lobster is cleaned in water with a brush, by taking hold of its back with the left hand and using the brush with the right. In this way it is harmless. The water is brought to boil in the meantime with salt and the 12 pepper-corns, then the lobsters are put in head first, which kills them instantly. Boil 5 minutes, then set aside to simmer 45 minutes. After this time take out the lobsters, dry them and put them on a board, break off the claws and tail and split the body into halves from head to tail. Arrange these halves upright on a platter, put a bunch of parsley in the top, place lettuce leaves around and garnish neatly with the tails, cracked claws and legs.

Creamed butter or butter balls are served with it, also a mayonnaise dressing.

Remarks: Claws and legs are placed into a cloth and carefully cracked so the meat is not crushed. Large lobsters may boil 1 hour.

No. 49—COLD LOBSTER.

Quantity for 6 Persons.

Preparation and ingredients are the same as in the preceding, No. 48. When the lobster is done, pour a cupful of cold water into the hot water and let the lobster cool in it. Then take it out, dry it and press it under a heavy board for one hour. When serving, brush it with oil and prepare it like the warm lobster. A mayonnaise dressing is nice with it.

No. 50—LOBSTER CROQUETTES OR CUTLETS.

Quantity for 6 Persons.

Utilizing remnants of lobsters.

The preparation and ingredients are the same as those given under No. 38 and 39, Fish Croquettes or Cutlets.

No. 51—LOBSTER RAGOUT IN SHELLS OR ON TOAST.

Quantity for 6 Persons.

2 lobsters, 3 lbs.
⅛ lb. of butter
2 tbsps. of flour
½ pt. bouillon
1 tsp. of meat extract
1 pinch of salt
1 pinch of pepper
1 pinch of sugar
1 tbsp. of lemon juice
4 pepper-corns
1 clove
¼ bay-leaf
⅛ of an onion
2 tbsps. of Madeira
⅛ pt. of white wine
¼ pt. of champignons
3 truffles
1 cup tomatoes

Preparation: The lobster is prepared as given under No. 48. After the lobster is cooked, all meat is picked out, reserving the coral, which is pulverized. The ⅛ lb. of butter is browned with the flour, bouillon or water added and the coral put in. Meat extract, salt, pepper, sugar, lemon juice, cloves, bay-leaf, onion, Madeira, white wine and tomatoes added and smooth. It is strained and must be about ¾ of a pint, this is all cooked ½ hour. This gravy must be very savory. The champignons are cut into small pieces, the truffles peeled and chopped, then add the champignons, truffles and lobster to the strained gravy. This mixture is filled into buttered shells or small molds and baked in the oven for 5 to 10 minutes. Serve on slices of toast.

Remarks: This is a fine side dish.

No. 52—BAKED LOBSTER.

Quantity for 6 Persons.

The preparation and ingredients are the same as given under No. 48. When the lobster is cooked and split, hot butter is dripped on and the lobster baked in it for 10 to 15 minutes.

A mayonnaise dressing and chopped pickles are nice with it.

Remarks: It is best to bake the lobster in a gas oven.

No. 53—BOILED CRAWFISH OR CRABS.

Quantity for 6 Persons.

24 crabs
Sufficient water
2 tbsps. of caraway
Salt
1 large onion, sliced

The Gravy.

⅛ lb. of butter
2 tbsps. of chopped parsley

Preparation: The crabs are cleaned like the lobster. See No. 48. The water with caraway seeds, salt and sliced onion is boiled and the crabs put in one by one. The water must boil constantly, so that the crabs are killed instantly. Boil 3 minutes, then set aside to simmer ¾ to 1 hour. Serve the hot crabs on a napkin. For gravy or dressing, take hot butter mixed with minced parsley.

No. 54—CRAB CUTLETS WITH VEGETABLES.

Quantity for 6 Persons.

36 crabs
1 oz. of butter

2 yolks of eggs
1 egg
Salt, pepper
1 tsp. of lemon juice
1 cupful of roll crumbs
½ lb. of butter for frying

Preparation: The crabs are prepared and cooked as given under No. 53. The meat picked out, 18 claws or legs laid aside. The meat is coarsely minced, then mixed well with creamed butter, 2 yolks of eggs, lemon juice, salt and pepper and small croquettes made from this mixture. Dip in beaten egg and roll crumbs. Heat the butter and fry these croquettes in it on both sides to a nice color. Into each put a claw or leg. Arrange the croquettes around asparagus or peas.

Remarks: A good crab dressing may be prepared from the meat of crabs.

No. 55—CRAB RAGOUT.

Quantity for 6 Persons.

50 crabs
¼ lb. of butter
3 tbsps. of flour
1 pt. bouillon
Some champignon water
¼ wineglassful of white wine
1 tbsp. of lemon juice
1 pinch of salt and pepper
2 yolks of eggs
½ pt. champignons

Preparation: The crabs or crawfish are cooked the same way as given under No. 53, the meat all picked out, also out of the tails and cut into small pieces. The coral is pulverized and cooked in ¼ lb. of butter together with flour browned in it. The bouillon, the champignon juice, white wine, lemon juice, salt and pepper are added and cooked for 15 minutes in a covered pan. This gravy is then strained through a fine sieve and the crab meat and champignons put in. This mixture is filled into shells or patties and baked in oven 5 minutes. (See Chapter 3, No. 29., Veal Sweetbread Patties). You can also serve this ragout on toast.

No. 56—OYSTERS.

Quantity for 6 Persons.

6 doz. oysters
1½ lemon

Preparation: The oysters are opened with an oyster knife and cleaned with a small knife, then placed neatly on a platter covered with a napkin, garnishing with slices of lemon.

No. 57—OYSTER PATTIES.

Quantity for 6 Persons.

2½ doz. oysters
1 tbsp. of butter
1 tbsp. of flour
1 tsp. of lemon juice
Salt, pepper
Pie crust
2 tbsps. of cream

Preparation: The butter is melted, flour, cream, lemon juice, salt, pepper and oysters put in, then boiled up once. Small patties are made as given under Chapter 3, No. 29, Veal Sweet Bread Patties. Fill the patties with the oyster ragout, bake in oven a few minutes, then serve at once. This is a fine dish.

No. 58—FRIED OYSTERS OR CLAMS.

Quantity for 6 Persons.

3 doz. oysters
Salt, pepper
1 cupful of fine roll crumbs
⅛ lb. of butter
Some lemon juice

Preparation: The prepared oysters are put into a dish, the lemon juice dripped on and breaded with crumbs, which are mixed with salt and pepper. In the meantime brown the butter and fry the oysters crisp, turning frequently. Serve them with spinage, sauerkraut and fish.

No. 59—OYSTER OR CLAM SALAD.

Quantity for 6 Persons.

50 oysters or clams
Juice of 2 lemons
Salt, white pepper
2 tbsps. of chopped parsley
4 tbsps. of oil

Preparation: The oysters or clams are mixed with the other ingredients, put into a glass dish and garnished with green lettuce leaves.

No. 60—OYSTER OR CLAM PUDDING WITH RICE.

Quantity for 6 Persons.

50 clams
1 pt. white wine
1 tsp. of salt

For the Rice.

¼ lb. of rice
1 pt. bouillon

For the Gravy.

¼ lb. of butter
3 tbsps. of flour
¾ pt. cream or milk
1 tbsp. of lemon juice
3 yolks of egg
½ tbsp. of Parmesan cheese
2 tbsps. chopped champignons

Preparation: The clams are cleaned in cold water with a brush. Change the water several times until it remains clear.

The white wine and salt are put into a dish and the clams put in and shaken over the fire until they open. The inside is then taken out, the shells thrown away. The clam liquor is used for dressing or gravy. Heat ¼ lb. of butter, stir in the flour and add cream, the liquor from the clams, chopped champignons and let it boil a few minutes, stirring constantly; then stir in the 3 yolks of eggs and set aside.

While the clams and dressing are being prepared, the rice is cooked with the bouillon to a thick mush.

A baking dish or casserole is buttered and filled with layers of rice alternating with layers of clams, rice for the top layer. The prepared gravy or dressing is then poured on, cheese strewn over, 1 tablespoonful of hot butter dripped on and then baked in the oven for 20 minutes. This dish may also be made of fresh oysters.

No. 61—SALMON STEAK.

Quantity for 6 Persons.

2½–3 lbs. of salmon in 6 slices
9 tsps. of lemon juice
2 medium-sized onions
1 bunch of parsley
Pepper 12 tbsps. of fine oil
Salt

Preparation: The steaks should be cut in 6 neat medium-sized pieces from the middle of the fish, sprinkle with salt and pepper, pour 1½ tablespoonfuls of lemon juice on each steak, the onion must be thinly sliced, and the slices put on the steaks, also the parsley; then spread 1 tablespoonful of oil on each steak and let them lie for 1½ hours; get cooking utensil very hot, then remove the onions and parsley from each slice of fish, spread another tablespoonful of oil on each and broil for 5 minutes. Serve on a hot platter and garnish with lemon slices and parsley. An olive sauce should be served with this dish.

HEAD CHEESE AND GELATINES.

The various preparations of Gelatines, Aspic, Headcheese, Poultry and Fish Jellies.

No. 1—HOW TO PREPARE GELATINE.

4 lbs. of pork sward or skin
4 lbs. of pig's feet
6 qts. of water
7 whites of eggs and the shells
1 qt. of white wine
Juice of 3 lemons

Preparation: The pork sward and pig's feet are cleaned well in cold water, then put in cold water and brought to boil. As soon as they begin to boil, pour this water off and cut the sward up into small pieces, chop the feet into several pieces and put on the stove with 6 qts. of cold water to boil for 7 hours. The feet may be taken out before this time if you wish to use them for a meal. The broth must boil down to 2½ qts.; this is strained through a fine sieve, set aside to cool, and all fat removed from the top.

Whites of eggs, wine and lemon juice are thoroughly beaten together; the egg shells are crushed and all this put into the broth. Then put the broth over the fire once more and stir constantly until it boils. Remove at once, cover up the pot and place it in a moderate oven until the liquid is perfectly clarified. Put a clean white cloth over a pot and strain the broth through it. This must be as clear as water. Put into glass jars, seal and set them in a boiler with water at the bottom, the jars resting on a tray. Cover the kettle and boil for 1 hour. This gelatine will keep and may be used for sweet or sour gelatines.

Remarks: The pig's feet may be served with a brown sweet-sour gravy. They may be eaten cold if put in vinegar, onion slices, salt and pepper-corns for 2 days.

No. 2—MEAT GELATINE FOR PATIENTS.

Quantity 1½ qts.

1 lb. of beef
2½ lbs. veal cartilage
Salt
¾ qt. of water
1 small carrot

Preparation: The beef and the veal cartilage are washed and cut into small pieces, the carrot is scraped, but left whole. Then this meat, the carrot and 1 pinch of salt are put into a glass jar with ¾ qt. of water, sealed and slowly cooked in a boiler with water at the bottom, the jar resting on a tray, for 4 hours. After that, strain the broth, let it get cold and remove the fat, then serve it to the patient in spoonfuls.

Remarks: Instead of beef, you may use poultry.

No. 3—GELATINE OR HEADCHEESE FROM POULTRY BOUILLON.

Quantity for 4–6 Persons.

1 young, fried or boiled chicken
¾ qt. good beef bouillon
2 tbsps. of Madeira or white wine
½ tsp. of meat extract
5 layers of ½ box of white gelatine
2 sour pickles.

Preparation: The fried chicken is cut into small pieces, the pickles are peeled and sliced. The strong beef broth is heated and the gelatine dissolved in it with wine, meat extract and salt added, then strained and tasted as to seasoning. Put ¼ pt. of the warm fluid into a porcelain dish, skim off all fat, let it get cold and put on the sliced pickles and a few tablespoonfuls of broth, let it cool, arrange the chicken meat on it in the form of scales, pour the rest of the broth on and let it get cold and stiff. Then turn it out on a platter and garnish with parsley. Asparagus cut into small pieces may also be used in this gelatine.

Remarks: Instead of chicken you may use veal roast, tongue or goose liver from which all hard fried meat and cartilage is removed.

No. 4—HEADCHEESE FROM PIG'S FEET AND CALF'S TONGUE.

Quantity for 6 Persons.

4 pig's feet
2 calves' tongues
Juice of ½ lemon
⅛ pt. of white wine
3 tbsps. of vinegar
Some salt
2 qts. of water
1 small onion
½ bay-leaf
¼ tsp. of meat extract
1 sour pickle, cut into small pieces
4 pepper-corns

Preparation: Pig's feet and calves' tongues are cleaned well, put on to boil with the water, salt, pepper, onion, bay-leaf. Cover the pot and boil until well done, then take the skin off the tongue and cut it with the rest of the meat into small pieces.

Strain the bouillon and add vinegar, lemon juice, wine and meat extract. Put the meat into a dish, pour the bouillon on and set to cool. Then turn it out on a platter and serve with head lettuce or potato salad, vinegar and oil, mayonnaise dressing or with fried potatoes.

No. 5—HEADCHEESE FROM OX-TONGUE.

Quantity for 6 Persons.

1 pickled ox-tongue
½ qt. strong beef bouillon
4 pieces of white gelatine
1 tbsp. of capers
4 sliced pickles
½ pt. sliced champignons
⅛ pt. white wine
Some champignon water
½ tsp. of meat extract
Some vinegar

Preparation: The tongue is cleaned and put on to boil in cold water until tender. It is then skinned and sliced, ½ pt. of vinegar poured on and left for a few hours. The bouillon is seasoned with salt, wine, champignon juice, lemon juice, some vinegar and the 4 pieces of gelatine are dissolved in the bouillon. The tongue, champignon and pickle slices and capers are put into a porcelain dish, the bouillon poured on and cooled; then turned out on a platter and served.

No. 6—HEADCHEESE FROM GOOSE OR DUCK.

Quantity for 6 Persons.

1 goose, 8 to 10 lbs.
6 calves' feet

For Cooking.

6 qts. of water
Salt
6 pepper-corns
2 cloves
1 bay-leaf
1 large sliced onion
Some soup greens
1 tsp. of meat extract
½ cup of good vinegar
4 whites of eggs and shells

Preparation: The goose and calves' feet are cleaned and well jointed, then put to boil in cold water with all the other ingredients. When the goose is tender, take it out of the broth, remove all spices that may adhere to it, place it into a porcelain or stone jar. Let the calves' feet cook until boiled down to 3 qts., remove all fat and season with vinegar, meat extract and salt if necessary. Put in the crushed egg shells, beat the white of egg with water and add it to the bouillon, let it come to boil and then set aside to simmer until the white of egg curdles. After one hour, strain the bouillon and pour it through a white cloth over the goose meat.

Remarks: If you wish to prepare the headcheese quickly, omit the calves' feet and use 35 pieces of gelatine dissolved in 3 qts. of bouillon, which is also clarified with white of egg and egg shells.

Remarks: The meat of the calves' feet may be breaded in roll crumbs, fried in butter and served with a raisin gravy. If you wish to make this headcheese from duck, take 2 ducks.

No. 7—HEAD CHEESE FROM PARTRIDGE.

Quantity for 6 Persons.

3 partridges
2 qts. of water

Salt
4 pepper-corns
½ onion
2 cloves
1 bay-leaf
2 tbsps. of lemon juice
4 tbsps. of Madeira or good white wine
2 whites of eggs and egg shells
15 pieces of gelatine or 1⁄20 of a lb.
¼ tsp. of meat extract

Preparation: The partridges are cleaned and dressed and put to boil in cold water with the spices. When it is done, carve it and put it into a porcelain dish. Let the bouillon boil down to 1¼ qts., season with white wine or Madeira, lemon juice and meat extract and remove all fat, then dissolve the gelatine in it. Stir the whites of eggs with some bouillon and add it with the egg shells, then boil for a few minutes and set aside to simmer until the bouillon is clear. Strain it through a sieve and a cloth and pour it on to the meat to cool. Turn it out on a platter and garnish with lettuce and lemon slices.

No. 8—FISH IN JELLY.

Quantity for 6 Persons.

2½ lbs. of fish
2½ qts. of water
Salt
4 pepper-corns
2 cloves
2 lemon slices
2 tbsps. of vinegar
4 tbsps. of lemon juice
¼ pt. of white wine
10 pieces of white gelatine
1 bay-leaf

Preparation: Put the water on with all the other ingredients and boil, then put in the fish after being dressed and cleaned and let it simmer gently for ½ hour. Take out the fish, remove the bones and cut it up into large pieces. The fish stock is boiled down to 1¼ qts. and the gelatine dissolved in it, then boiled for one hour, strained and poured on the fish to cool. Serve it on a glass platter garnished with head lettuce.

No. 9—EEL IN JELLY.

Quantity for 6 Persons.

3 lbs. of eel
1½ qts. of water
¼ qt. of wine vinegar
10 pepper-corns
3 cloves
Salt
2 bay-leaves
1 sliced onion
Some soup greens
¼ lemon, sliced
12 layers of white gelatine
¼ tsp. of meat extract
2 hard-boiled eggs
White of 1 egg

Preparation: The eel is skinned, cut in pieces and the intestines taken out. The 1½ qts. of water are brought to boil with vinegar, pepper-corns, salt, bay-leaf, onions, lemon slices and soup greens; add the eel and simmer gently for 15 minutes. Take out the pieces of eel and boil the broth down to 1 qt. Into this put the crushed egg shells, the white of egg mixed with some broth, ¼ teaspoonful of meat extract and the gelatine and cook for a minute, then set aside. When the bouillon is clear, strain it through a fine cloth. Slice the two hard boiled eggs and cover the bottom of a porcelain dish with them, then pour on some jelly and fish bouillon and let it get cold. After that put the eel pieces on and the rest of the sliced egg, then pour the rest of the stock over and let it get cold. When it is stiff, turn it out on a plate and garnish with head lettuce, It is best to prepare this dish the day before using it.

No. 10—SALMON IN JELLY.

Quantity for 6 Persons.

2½ lbs. of salmon
1½ qts. of water
½ cup of wine vinegar
1 cup of white wine
½ sliced onion
¼ sliced lemon
12 pepper-corns
5 cloves
2 bay-leaves
10 pieces of gelatine
2 whites of eggs and shells
10 crab tails if you like
Salt

Preparation: Into the water put the wine vinegar, the wine, salt, pepper-corns, bay-leaves, cloves, onion slices, lemon slices and let it come to boil. Clean the fish well and put it into this water to simmer gently for ½ to ¾ hour. After this take the fish out, remove the bones, cut in pieces and boil down the stock to 1 qt. Beat the whites of 2 eggs with some of the broth and add it, also the crushed shells and 10 pieces or layers of gelatine. Let this mass cook a second and set aside to clarify, then strain through a fine cloth.

Place the pieces of fish and crab tails into a porcelain dish, pour the fish stock on and put it on ice to cool quickly. Then turn it out on a glass platter and garnish with head lettuce and lemon slices. Serve with a mayonnaise dressing.

No. 11—OYSTERS AND CAVIAR IN JELLY.

Quantity for 6 Persons.

1 qt. strong beef bouillon
3 tbsps. of white wine
1 tsp. of lemon juice
12 layers of gelatine
4 doz. oysters
¼ lb. of caviar, ice
2 whites of eggs and shells

Preparation: The beef bouillon must be clear and free from fat; season it with white wine and lemon juice, and dissolve the gelatine in it. Stir the white of egg with some bouillon and add it, put in the crushed egg shells to cook for a second, then set aside to clarify. Strain it through a fine cloth. Fresh oysters are opened, cleaned and cut out of the shells. A dish is set on chopped ice, some oysters are placed in a circle into the dish and sufficient cold bouillon put on to cover; then let them get stiff. Repeat this until all oysters have been used. Put the rest of the bouillon on top and let it get stiff.

The caviar is poured into a sieve, let very cold water run over it until it becomes granular. In the center of the oyster jelly cut out a round hole, large enough to hold the quantity of caviar at hand. Heat the oyster jelly that has been cut out and pour it over the caviar. When it is perfectly stiff, turn it out on a platter and garnish with lemon slices and lettuce leaves. Serve with a cold mustard dressing.

No. 12—GOOSE LIVER IN JELLY.

Quantity for 6 Persons.

1½ lbs. of fat goose liver
¼ lb. of truffles
¼ lb. of champignons
¾ qt. very strong beef or chicken broth
½ tsp. of meat extract

3 tbsps. of Madeira
10 pieces of white gelatine
1 white of egg and shell for clearing

Preparation: Remove all fat from the broth. Dissolve the gelatine in it, color with the meat extract and season with Madeira. Add to it the white of egg beaten into some of the broth, and the crushed shell, cook a second and set aside to clarify, then strain through a fine cloth.

Skin the goose liver and cut it into 1½ inch slices, also the truffles and lard the liver slices with the truffles, then stew slowly in a little butter. When done, place them on blotting paper to drain off the fat. The champignons are cooked in bouillon for 10 minutes.

Into a dish set in crushed ice put part of the bouillon, let it get stiff and put in half of the goose liver, also half of the champignons. Some more bouillon is poured over this and cooled; then repeat this same process until all goose liver, champignons and broth have been used. Let it get stiff, turn it out on a platter and serve with a cold mustard dressing and potato salad.

DRESSINGS or GRAVIES.

DRESSINGS FOR MEAT, POULTRY, GAME AND FISH.

SAUCES FOR PASTRY AND SWEET DISHES.

Flour Gravies.

Good butter and good flour are the essentials for a gravy and constitute the main part of it. For the preparation of white gravies, earthen, pewter or enameled dishes are the best. Gravies must always be smooth and it is best to strain them through a fine sieve. If you have them ready before the meal, put them into a double boiler. They must neither be too thick nor too thin.

No. 1—WHITE GRAVY.

Quantity for 6 Persons.

1 oz. butter
¼ small onion
2 tbsps. of flour
¾ pt. of bouillon
1 pinch of salt and pepper
2 yolks of eggs

Preparation: Melt the butter, add the peeled onion and steep a little while, then stir in the flour and bouillon and cook 10 minutes, season with salt and pepper. Beat the 2 yolks of eggs with a little water and slowly stir it into the gravy. Do not boil any more.

No. 2—DUTCH GRAVY.

For Fish, Chicken or Veal With Rice.

Quantity for 6 Persons.

1 oz. of butter
2 tbsps. of flour
½ pt. of fish stock, chicken or veal broth
1½ tsps. of lemon juice, for fish
2 tbsps. white wine, for chicken
Salt
2 yolks of eggs
¼ cup of cream

Preparation: Melt the butter, stir in the flour, stew a few minutes, fill up with fish stock, stirring constantly, then season with salt and lemon juice and add the 2 yolks of eggs as given under No. 1.

Remarks: If the gravy is for chicken or veal with rice, season it with white wine.

No. 3—FINE DUTCH GRAVY FOR FISH OR VEAL.

Quantity for 6 Persons.

1 oz. of butter
2 tbsps. of flour
½ pt. fish stock or bouillon.
½ cup sour cream
1 tbsp. of lemon juice
1 tbsp. of capers
3 sardines
Salt
1 pinch of white pepper
2 yolks of eggs

Preparation: Melt the butter, stir in the flour, simmer gently, fill up with fish stock, or bouillon if it is intended for veal. Cook, stirring constantly, add sour cream, lemon juice, salt and pepper.

The sardines are cleaned, chopped and put into the gravy with the capers. Cook slowly for ten minutes, stirring frequently, then strain through a fine sieve, heat it again and add the 2 yolks of eggs.

No. 4—WHIPPED DUTCH GRAVY.

For Fish, Asparagus, Cauliflower, Oyster Plants and Scorzonera.

Quantity for 6 Persons.

½ pt. of fish stock for fish, or ½ pt. of vegetable broth for vegetables
1 oz. of butter
3–4 yolks of eggs
Salt, pepper
1½ tbsps. of flour

Preparation: The flour is mixed well with fish stock or vegetable broth and whipped while over the fire, until it thickens; then add the fresh butter and the yolks of eggs, which have been beaten with water. Let it boil, stirring constantly. Serve at once.

Remarks: The gravy may be seasoned with 1 teaspoonful of lemon juice.

No. 5—GOOD FISH GRAVY.

Quantity for 6 Persons.

1 oz. of butter
2 tbsps. of flour
⅓ pt. of fish stock
2–3 yolks of eggs
Juice of ½ lemon
Salt
½ cup of cream

Preparation: Melt the butter, stir in the flour, add the fish stock and cream and cook a little while, stirring constantly, then season with lemon juice and salt if necessary. Finally stir in the yolks of eggs.

No. 6—CAULIFLOWER GRAVY.

Quantity for 6 Persons.

1 oz. of butter
2 tbsps. of flour
½ pt. of cauliflower broth
Salt to taste
2 yolks of eggs
Nutmeg to taste

Preparation: Melt the butter, stir in the flour, gradually pour in the cauliflower broth and boil, stirring constantly. Then season with salt and nutmeg and stir in the 2 yolks of eggs.

No. 7—ASPARAGUS GRAVY.

Quantity for 6 Persons.

⅛ lb. of butter
1 tbsp. of flour
4–6 yolks of eggs
½ cup of cream
⅓ pt. of asparagus broth
Salt to taste

Preparation: Cream the butter, add the yolks of eggs, flour and cream; then add the boiling asparagus broth, while stirring. Let it boil, stirring constantly. Serve at once or keep warm in water. It is very fine.

No. 8—FINE MUSTARD GRAVY.

For Beef and Fish.

Quantity for 6 Persons.

⅛ lb. of butter
3 yolks of eggs
2 tbsps. of mustard
1 tbsp. of flour
1 tbsp. of lemon juice
1 slice of lemon
1 pinch of sugar
1 pinch of salt
½ pt. bouillon

Preparation: Cream the butter, add the yolks of eggs, mustard, flour, and gradually pour in the bouillon, stirring constantly, then cook. Season it with lemon juice, sugar and salt if necessary. Put in the lemon slice which should be taken out when served.

No. 9—PLAIN MUSTARD DRESSING.

For Fish and Beef.

Quantity for 6 Persons.

1⁄10 lb. of butter
1½ tbsps. of flour
2 tbsps. of mustard
1 tbsp. of vinegar
1 pinch of salt
Sugar, pepper
½ pt. of bouillon

Preparation: Brown the butter and flour, add the bouillon, cook and season with pepper, salt, sugar and vinegar.

No. 10—FINE BEARNAISE SAUCE.

For Fillets, Saddle of Mutton, Mutton Cutlets.

Quantity for 6 Persons.

1 leek
3 tbsp. of vinegar
¼ lb. of butter
4 yolks of eggs
¼ cup of bouillon
½ tsp. of meat extract
1½ tsps. of chopped parsley
Salt, pepper

Preparation: The leek is cut into small pieces, vinegar added, then boiled down to one-half of the portion and strained through a fine sieve. Cream the butter, stir in the yolks of eggs, the leek vinegar, meat extract and bouillon. Place into a double boiler and let it thicken, stirring constantly; season with salt, pepper and finely chopped parsley. It must be smooth. Serve at once.

No. 11—TOMATO GRAVY.

For Fillet, Saddle of Mutton and Mutton Cutlets.

Quantity for 6 Persons.

1 leek
3 tbsps. of vinegar
⅛ lb. of butter
3 yolks of eggs
¼ cup of bouillon
¼ cup of tomato pulp
1 tsp. of sugar
Salt, pepper
½ tsp. of flour

Preparation: The leek is cut into small pieces and boiled down in vinegar to half of the portion. Cream the butter, add yolks of eggs, tomatoes, flour, bouillon and the strained leek vinegar. Put into a double boiler and let it thicken, stirring constantly. Season with sugar, salt and pepper and serve at once.

No. 12—FINE TOMATO DRESSING.

Quantity for 6 Persons.

1 oz. of butter
1½ tbsps. of flour
1 lb. or ¼ qt. can of tomatoes
¼ lb. raw ham
½ onion
1 pt. bouillon
Salt to taste
1 pinch of sugar and pepper
½ tbsp. of lemon juice
2 yolks of eggs

Preparation: Ham and onion are cut into fine pieces and fried brown in butter. The chopped tomatoes are added and cooked a little while; then stir in the flour and add the bouillon. Season it with salt, pepper, lemon juice and sugar. Cook the gravy slowly for 1 hour, strain through a fine sieve and stir in the 2 yolks of eggs.

No. 13—FINE GRAVY.

For Poultry, Meat and Fish.

Quantity for 6 Persons.

⅛ lb. of butter
⅛ lb. of raw ham
1 small onion

1½ tbsps. of flour
⅓ pt. bouillon
⅓ pt. cream or milk
¼ cup of ground poultry, fish or meat
Salt, pepper
1 tsp. of lemon juice

Preparation: The lean ham is cut into small cubes and fried in the butter. Add the sliced onion, stir in the flour and stew a little while, add the bouillon and cream. Now the gravy is cooked for 15 minutes and the ¼ cupful of ground fish added. When served with meats, add meat instead of fish. Season with salt, pepper and lemon juice. Let it boil a while and strain through a fine sieve.

No. 14—HORSE RADISH GRAVY.

Quantity for 6 Persons.

½ cup of horse radish
1½ tsps. of flour
1 tbsp. of butter
¾ cup of cream or bouillon
1 pinch of salt
1 tsp. of sugar

Preparation: The horse radish must be scraped and grated very quickly, flour and butter stirred in and the cream added. Let it boil 15 to 20 minutes, stirring constantly, and season with salt and sugar.

No. 15—HORSE RADISH DRESSING, RAW.

Quantity for 6 Persons.

½ cup of horse radish
3 tbsps. of vinegar

1 pinch of salt
1 tsp. of sugar

Preparation: The prepared horse radish is mixed with vinegar, salt and sugar and served that way.

No. 16—SARDINE GRAVY.

For Fish and Meat.

Quantity for 6 Persons.

⅛ lb. of butter
2 tbsps. of flour
½ pt. of strong bouillon or fish stock
¼ pt. of white wine
Juice of ½ lemon
4–6 sardines
Salt
1 pinch of pepper
2 yolks of eggs

Preparation: The sardines are soaked in water for ½ hour, then chopped fine and rubbed through a sieve. Melt the butter, stir in the flour and stew a while, then add the bouillon, or fish stock if used for fish. Add wine and lemon juice and the sardines, cook it slowly for 15 minutes and season with salt and pepper; then stir in the yolks of eggs, but do not boil it any longer.

No. 17—CAPER SAUCE.

Quantity for 6 Persons.

1⁄10 lb. of butter
¼ of an onion
1½ tbsps. of flour

¾ pt. of bouillon (or fish stock, for fish)
2 tbsps. of capers
1 tbsp. of lemon juice
Salt
1 pinch of pepper
2 yolks of eggs

Preparation: Melt the butter, add the sliced onion and stew a while, then stir in the flour and add the bouillon, season with salt, pepper, lemon juice, and boil 15 minutes, stirring constantly. Strain through a fine sieve. Put in the capers and let it simmer gently. Stir in the yolks of eggs and a pinch of sugar.

No. 18—OYSTER DRESSING.

Quantity for 6 Persons.

18 oysters
1/10 lb. of butter
1½ tbsps. of flour
1 pt. strong bouillon
1 sardine or 1 tbsp. sardine butter
1 pinch of salt
Pepper
½ cup of cream

Preparation: Melt the butter, stir in the flour, add the bouillon, and oyster liquor. If the oysters are fresh, you may use some of the beards. Cook the gravy slowly for ½ hour, then strain through a fine sieve and season with salt and pepper. Put in the sardine butter or finely chopped sardines. The oysters are put into boiling water for ¼ minute, then placed into a colander to drain. Put into the hot gravy and serve at once.

No. 19—CRAB OR LOBSTER GRAVY.

For Fish, Chicken and Fricassee.

Quantity for 6 Persons.

18 crabs
2 qts. salt water
1⁄10 lb. of butter
2 tbsps. of flour
Salt
1 pinch of pepper
Sugar
2 tbsps. of cream
½ pt. of rich bouillon

Preparation: The crabs are brushed well in cold water, then cooked very red in 2 qts. of boiling salt water. The claws and tails are broken off and the meat picked out and cut up. Remove the gravy substance from the bodies and crush the coral in a mortar.

Heat the butter and put in the crushed coral, stir while stewing, add the 2 tablespoonfuls of flour, stew a while and add the bouillon, cook it slowly until it is smooth, then strain through a sieve and season with salt and pepper. Stir in the 2 tablespoonfuls of cream, let the gravy get very hot and put in the meat from the tails and claws. It must not boil any more.

Lobster gravy is prepared the same way. Instead of crabs or crab butter, take lobsters or lobster butter.

Remarks: A left over body of a lobster may be utilized for a gravy.

No. 20—REMOULADE SAUCE.

Quantity for 6 Persons.

3 tbsps. of fine oil
1½ tbsps. of flour
½ pt. of bouillon
2 hard-boiled yolks of eggs

1 raw yolk of egg
1½ tbsps. of lemon juice
1 tsp. of mustard
Salt
1 pinch of pepper
½ tsp. of sugar

Preparation: Stew the oil and flour a little while, add the bouillon, cook, strain and stir until cold. Stir the hard-boiled yolks of eggs together with the raw yolk, lemon juice, mustard and gradually stir in the oil mixture. Season with salt, pepper and sugar. It is served with beef, eggs and head cheese.

No. 21—WHITE FRICASSEE SAUCE.

For Chicken Fricassee or Veal Fricassee.

Quantity for 6 Persons.

1 small piece of butter
2 tbsps. of flour
1 pt. bouillon
1 tbsp. of lemon juice
Salt
1 pinch of pepper
½ wineglass of white wine

Preparation: Melt the butter and stir in the flour, add the bouillon, stir and boil 5 minutes, add white wine, lemon juice, salt, pepper and set to simmer gently.

No. 22—ONION GRAVY.

For Boiled Beef.

Quantity for 6 Persons.

1 small piece of butter
1 medium-sized onion
1 tbsp. of flour
Salt
1 pinch of pepper
1 tbsp. of vinegar
½ pt. bouillon

Preparation: Brown the butter with the sliced onion, stir in the flour, add the bouillon and season with salt, vinegar and pepper. Cook the gravy 10 minutes and strain through a fine sieve.

No. 23—PEARL ONION GRAVY.

Quantity for 6 Persons.

1 small piece of butter
½ tbsp. of sliced onion
1½ tbsp. of flour
½ pt. of bouillon
1½ tbsps. of vinegar
Salt
1 pinch of pepper
2 yolks of eggs
2 tbsps. of small pearl onions

Preparation: Prepare the gravy just like onion gravy, No. 22. After the gravy has been strained, put in the pearl onions, cook for 1 minute and stir in the yolks of eggs, but do not cook any longer.

No. 24—PICKLE GRAVY.

Quantity for 6 Persons.

1 piece of butter

2 tbsps. of sliced onion
1½ tbsps. of flour
¾ pt. of bouillon
¼ tsp. of meat extract
Salt, pepper
½ tbsp. of vinegar
1 tsp. of sugar
2 small chopped pickles

Preparation: Brown the butter, stir in the onion and flour, cook a minute, and add the bouillon. Add the meat extract and cook 15 minutes, then strain and season with salt, pepper, vinegar, sugar. Put in the finely chopped pickles and set to simmer. You can improve this gravy with pieces of cauliflower and small pearl onions. Serve with mutton roast or lamb.

No. 25—BURGUNDY OR MADEIRA SAUCE.

For Ham, Fish or Tongue.

Quantity for 6 Persons.

1⁄10 lb. of butter
2 tbsps. of flour
¾ pt. of bouillon
1 cup of Burgundy, red wine or Madeira
Salt
1 clove
1 bay-leaf
1 lemon slice
1 tbsp. lemon juice
1 tsp. sugar
½ tsp. meat extract
6 pepper-corns

Preparation: Brown the butter and flour, add the bouillon and all the other ingredients.

Cook this gravy for 1 hour slowly, stirring frequently, then strain through a fine sieve, add a few tablespoonfuls of wine, season and serve hot. It must be a nice brown color and smooth.

No. 26—BACON GRAVY.

Quantity for 6 Persons.

⅛ lb. of bacon
2 tbsps. of flour
¾ pt. bouillon
¼ onion
Salt
6 pepper-corns
1 clove
1 bay-leaf
2 tbsps. of vinegar
Sugar

Preparation: Cut the bacon into small cubes and fry to a nice yellow color, add the finely sliced onion and fry a little while, add the flour and bouillon and season with salt, pepper, cloves, bay-leaf, vinegar and sugar. Cook for 15 minutes and serve with potatoes in their jackets.

No. 27—HERB GRAVY.

Quantity for 6 Persons.

3 tbsps. of minced herbs
1 tbsp. of minced parsley
1 tsp. of minced onions
1 spray of thyme
6 pepper-corns
2 tbsps. of flour
1¼ pts. of bouillon

½ tsp. meat extract
1 tsp. lemon juice
Salt to taste
2 tbsps. of butter

Preparation: Parsley, onion, thyme, pepper-corns are fried in butter, the flour stirred in and browned; add the bouillon and meat extract and boil down to ½ the quantity, strain through a fine sieve, heat again and put in the herbs. Season with lemon juice and salt and stir in a small piece of butter.

No. 28—BROWN CHAMPIGNON SAUCE.

Quantity for 6 Persons.

1/12 lb. of butter
2 tbsps. of flour
1 tsp. of sliced onion
1 pt. of bouillon
1 tsp. of meat extract
½ cup champignon liquor
¼ cup of red wine or
4 tbsps. of Madeira
1 tbsp. lemon juice
Salt to taste
1 pinch of sugar
½ pt. of champignons

Preparation: Brown the butter, stir in flour and onion and cook 1 minute, add the bouillon and champignon liquor, season with meat extract, red wine or Madeira, lemon juice and cook for ½ hour. Strain the gravy, add the champignons, which may be quartered if they are too large, set aside to simmer gently. Now flavor with salt, sugar and lemon juice.

No. 29—TRUFFLE SAUCE.

Quantity for 6 Persons.

1⁄12 lb of butter
3 tbsps. of flour
1 tsp. of chopped onion
1 pt. bouillon or beef gravy
1 cup red wine
½ cup Madeira
2 cloves
1 bay-leaf
1 pinch of sugar
Salt to taste
1 small can of truffles
½ tsp. meat extract
6 pepper-corns

Preparation: Butter and onion are browned, flour stirred in and bouillon added, together with red wine, Madeira, pepper, meat extract, cloves, bay-leaf and put in the peelings of truffles, cook slowly for 1 hour, strain through a fine sieve. Chop the peeled truffles and add them, season with salt and a little sugar.

No. 30—MOREL SAUCE.

Quantity for 6 Persons.

1 lb. of fresh morels or ½ can of morels
1 pt. of bouillon
2 tbsps. of butter
2½ tbsps. of flour
1 tsp. onion
1 pinch of pepper
½ pt. morel liquor
½ tsp. meat extract
⅛ lb. raw, lean ham
1 tsp. minced parsley

1 tsp. of butter
Salt

Preparation: The fresh morels are cleaned, washed in lukewarm water and put on the fire with lukewarm water, stirring carefully while heating the water. Then they are poured into a colander. This process is repeated until there is no more sand on the morels. The last water is put aside. After a while pour it off carefully from the settlings and boil down to ½ pt. The ham and onion are cut into small dice, fried brown in 2 tablespoonfuls of butter, the flour stirred in and browned 1 minute, then add the bouillon and morel liquor and cook slowly for 45 minutes. Add the meat extract, pepper, salt and strain it. Cut up the morels, put them into the gravy, let it come to boil again, add parsley and serve very hot.

No. 31—PARSLEY GRAVY.

Quantity for 6 Persons.

1⁄12 lb. of butter
1 tbsp. chopped onion
2½ tbsps. of flour
1 pt. bouillon
1 tbsp. of lemon juice
1 pinch of pepper
Salt
4 tbsps. of finely chopped parsley

Preparation: The finely chopped onions and flour are browned in butter, bouillon added and cooked 10 minutes, stirring constantly. Season with salt, pepper and lemon juice, add the chopped parsley, but do not cook any longer.

Remarks: ¼ cup of sweet cream will improve the gravy.

No. 32—DILL, CHIVE OR TARRAGON GRAVY.

These gravies are prepared like the parsley gravy, the ingredients are the same also, but instead of parsley take dill for dill gravy, chives for chive gravy, and tarragon for tarragon gravy. These gravies are good with fish, chicken, beef and asparagus.

No. 33—SORREL GRAVY.

Quantity for 6 Persons.

1⁄12 lb. of butter
2½ tbsps. of flour
1 pt. bouillon
½ cupful of sweet cream
2 yolks of eggs
½ tsp. of sugar
1 pinch of pepper
Salt to taste
½ cup of sorrel puree

Preparation: Melt the butter, stir in the flour, gradually add the bouillon and cream, stirring constantly, cook a few minutes and add the sorrel. Strain and season with salt, pepper and sugar. Stir in the yolks of eggs and serve very hot.

Remarks: The sorrel is cleaned and treated like spinage and boiled the same way, then rubbed through a sieve.

Cold Dressings.

No. 34—OIL DRESSING A LA TARTARE.

For Hard-Boiled Eggs, Cold Beef and Head Cheese.

Quantity for 6 Persons.

¼ cup of fine salad oil
1 tbsp. finely sliced onion
2 tbsps. of flour
½ pt. of bouillon
1½ tbsps. of minced herbs or minced mixed pickles
1 pinch of pepper
Salt to taste
Juice of ½ lemon

Preparation: Oil, onion and flour are fried light brown, bouillon and lemon juice added, cook a little while, then strain and stir until cold. Add the herbs or pickles and season with salt, pepper and more lemon juice, if necessary. If the gravy is too thick, when cold, add more bouillon.

No. 35—COLD MUSTARD DRESSING.

For Cold Lamb or Veal Roast.

Quantity for 6 Persons.

2 hard-boiled yolks of eggs
1 raw yolk of egg
½ cup of fine salad oil
Juice of ½ lemon
1 pinch of pepper
Sugar
1 tbsp. of cream
1 tbsp. of mustard
Salt to taste

Preparation: Hard-boiled and raw yolks of eggs are well stirred together, the oil added in drops, season with mustard, lemon juice, salt, pepper and sugar. If the dressing is too thick, thin it with 1 tablespoonful of cream. This dressing is very good with cold roast.

No. 36—TARTARE DRESSING.

Quantity for 6 Persons.

3 tbsps. of oil
2 tbsps. of flour
1 tbsp. of finely chopped onions
¾ pt. strong bouillon
1 tsp. mustard
Salt to taste
1 pinch of pepper
2 yolks of eggs
2 tbsps. of chopped mixed pickles
1 tbsp. of chopped capers
3 tbsps. lemon juice or vinegar

Preparation: Oil, onion, flour are fried light brown, bouillon added, seasoned with mustard, lemon juice, salt and pepper and cooked slowly for 15 minutes, then strained through a fine sieve. Stir until cold, then stir in the 2 yolks of eggs and the pickles and capers. Taste it again. It should be quite thick.

No. 37—COLD HERB DRESSING.

Quantity for 6 Persons.

2 hard-boiled eggs
1 raw yolk of egg
½ cup of fine salad oil
1½ tbsps. of minced herbs
1 mustardspoonful of mustard
1 tsp. of lemon juice or vinegar
Salt to taste
1 pinch of pepper

Preparation: The 2 hard-boiled and 1 raw yolk of eggs are thoroughly beaten together, the oil added a few drops at a time, the herbs and mustard put in and then seasoned with salt and pepper and the finely chopped white of egg put in also.

No. 38—COLD REMOULADE DRESSING.

Very fine.

Quantity for 6 Persons.

3 hard-boiled yolks of egg
2 raw yolks
¾ cup of fine salad oil
¼ cup thick sour cream
3 tbsps. lemon juice or vinegar
1 tbsp. chopped capers
¼ tbsp. chopped sardines
¼ tbsp. mustard
1 pinch of salt
Pepper

Preparation: The two kinds of yolks of eggs are mixed well, the oil added a few drops at a time, cream and lemon juice slowly stirred in, then capers, sardines and mustard are added. Season with salt and pepper and keep cold.

No. 39—COLD CHIVE DRESSING.

For Beef.

Quantity for 6 Persons.

½ cup of cream or milk
⅙ cup of vinegar
1 pinch of pepper and sugar
¼ cup of finely chopped chives
Salt to taste

Preparation: Cream, vinegar and chives are stirred together, then seasoned with salt, pepper and sugar.

No. 40—COLD CAVIAR DRESSING.

Quantity for 6 Persons.

½ lb. of caviar
3 yolks of eggs
½ cup of cream
2 tbsps. of vinegar
1 pinch of pepper and sugar
Salt to taste

Preparation: Put the 3 yolks of eggs and cream into a double boiler and cook until it thickens, stirring constantly, add the vinegar and stir until cold, then season with pepper, sugar and salt.

Put the caviar into a sieve, and let cold water run over it until it becomes granular, then stir into the dressing. This dressing is good with blue fish.

No. 41—MAYONNAISE DRESSING No. 1. (COLD).

Quantity for 6 Persons.

6 yolks of eggs
½ pt. olive oil
Juice of ¼ lemon
1/10 tsp. of mustard
¼ tsp. of sugar
Salt to taste
1 pinch of white pepper

Preparation: The 6 yolks of eggs are stirred with the oil, then seasoned with lemon juice, pepper, mustard, sugar and salt.

Remarks: Mayonnaise dressing is good with salmon.

No. 42—MAYONNAISE DRESSING No. 2.

Quantity for 6 Persons.

4 yolks of eggs
⅓ pt. fine salad oil
3 tbsps. of bouillon
2 tbsps. of vinegar
¼ tsp. of mustard
¼ tsp. of grated onion
1 pinch of pepper
Salt to taste

Preparation: The yolks of eggs are stirred adding the oil and vinegar a few drops at a time, season with onion, pepper and salt and add sufficient bouillon to give it the required thickness.

No. 43—COOKED MAYONNAISE DRESSING.

Very Good With Lobster or Chicken Salad.

Quantity for 6 Persons.

4 yolks of eggs
¾ cup of sour cream
2 tbsps. of vinegar
¼ tsp. ground mustard
1 pinch of white pepper
1 pinch of salt
1 pinch of sugar
½ pt. of thick, sour whipped cream

Preparation: Yolks of eggs, cream, vinegar, mustard, pepper, salt and sugar are mixed well and cooked in a double boiler, stirring constantly until it thickens. When the gravy is cold, add sour whipped cream.

Remarks: You may peel a dill pickle, chop it very fine and add to the dressing.

No. 44—MAYONNAISE DRESSING No. 3.

Very Good With Poultry Salad.

Quantity for 6 Persons.

4 yolks of eggs
1 tsp. of flour
1 cup of sweet cream
¼ cup of good poultry broth
1 pinch of white pepper
Salt
¼ tsp. of grated onion
2 tbsps. of fine oil
2 tbsps. of vinegar

Preparation: Yolks of eggs, cream, broth and vinegar are mixed well and boiled in double boiler as before mentioned in No. 43, then seasoned with salt, pepper and onion. Stir the dressing until cold, then add 2 tablespoonfuls of oil a few drops at a time.

Sweet Sauces or Dressings.

Sauces for Puddings and Pastries.

No. 45—WHITE WINE SAUCE.

Quantity for 6 Persons.

2 eggs

1 tsp. of flour
2 slices of lemon
2 tbsps. of sugar
1 tumblerful of white wine

Preparation: The 2 whole eggs, flour, wine, sugar are mixed well on the stove and stirred until it becomes foamy and begins to thicken, but must not cook. Then add the lemon slices.

Remarks: This sauce may be served cold or warm.

No. 46—ARRACK SAUCE.

Quantity for 6 Persons.

¼ cup of arrack or brandy
1 pt. of water
3 yolks of eggs
2 tbsps. of lemon juice
1 slice of lemon
1½ tbsps. of flour
⅛ lb. of sugar

Preparation: All ingredients except the arrack or brandy are mixed well and treated the same as mentioned under No. 45. The arrack or brandy is stirred in last. This sauce may be served cold or warm.

No. 47—VANILLA SAUCE.

Quantity for 6 Persons.

1 pt. of milk
½ vanilla bean or 1 tbsp. vanilla extract
4 yolks of eggs
1 tsp. of flour
¼ cup of sugar

Preparation: The vanilla bean is left to soak in milk for 1 hour, then the sugar is added. The milk is brought to boil, the yolks of eggs and flour are mixed with a little cold milk, slowly stirred into the boiling milk and cooked for one minute. If you wish to use this sauce cold, it must be stirred several times while getting cold so it will not form a skin.

Remarks: The sauce must be stirred well while boiling.

When it is used cold you may add ½ cup of whipped cream or the white of egg beaten to a froth.

No. 48—COCOA SAUCE.

Quantity for 6 Persons.

1 pt. milk
½ tsp. of vanilla extract
3 tbsps. of cocoa
¼ cup of sugar
4 yolks of eggs

Preparation: Stir the cocoa with the yolks of eggs and a little cold milk and prepare the sauce like vanilla sauce given under No. 47.

No. 49—CHOCOLATE SAUCE.

Quantity for 6 Persons.

The preparation is the same as given under No. 47 and No. 48, but instead of cocoa, ¼ lb. of chocolate is grated and stirred into the yolks of eggs and milk and less sugar is needed.

No. 50—LEMON SAUCE.

Quantity for 6 Persons.

1 pt. of milk
⅓ lemon peel
1 tsp. of flour
¼ cup of sugar
4 yolks of eggs

The preparation is the same as given under No. 47, but instead of vanilla use lemon peel.

No. 51—MARASCHINO SAUCE.

Quantity for 6 Persons.

4 tbsps. of maraschino
1 pt. of milk
1 tsp. of flour
¼ cup of sugar
4 yolks of eggs

The preparation is the same as given under No. 47, but instead of vanilla, use 4 tablespoonfuls maraschino.

Printed in the USA
CPSIA information can be obtained
at www.ICGtesting.com
LVHW080553211123
764513LV00010B/502

9 781835 524923